Critical Challenges in English
for Secondary Students

This series is one of a number of initiatives organized under the auspices of *TC²* — *The Critical Thinking Cooperative*. *TC²* is a partnership of British Columbia school districts, faculties of education, teacher professional associations, and other educational organizations. The aim of the cooperative is to promote critical thinking through partner-sponsored professional development, resource development and research activities. *TC²* functions as a clearinghouse and support network to promote critical thinking from primary to post-secondary education.

For more information about *TC²* contact:

LeRoi Daniels
The Critical Thinking Cooperative
c/o Richmond School District
7811 Granville Avenue
Richmond, British Columbia V6Y 3E3
Phone: (604) 732-1907   Fax: (604) 732-1957
e-mail: leroi.daniels@ubc.ca

Critical Challenges Across the Curriculum Series

Critical Challenges in English for Secondary Students

Editors

Samantha Butler
Holly Husarski
Nancy Shea

Contributing authors

Samantha Butler	Okanagan Similkameen School District
Suzanne Duke	West Vancouver School District
David Ellison	Abbotsford School District
Holly Husarski	Okanagan Similkameen School District
Larry Killick	Vancouver School District
Shani Laver	Okanagan Similkameen School District
Gale Parchoma	Okanagan Similkameen School District
Natasha Schroeter	Okanagan Similkameen School District
Nancy Shea	Okanagan Similkameen School District
Alan Stel	Okanagan Similkameen School District

 The Critical
Thinking
Cooperative

 Field Programs
Faculty of Education
Simon Fraser University

Series published by

The Critical Thinking Cooperative
c/o Richmond School District
7811 Granville Avenue
Richmond, British Columbia V6Y 3E3

Series produced by

Field Programs
Faculty of Education
Simon Fraser University
Burnaby, British Columbia, V5A 1S6

Design and Production: M. Kathie Wraight
Project Coordination: Patricia Holborn

Cover Design: Dynamic Desktop

Series distributed by

Pacific Educational Press
Faculty of Education
University of British Columbia
Vancouver, British Columbia, V6T 1Z4
Telephone: (604) 822-5385
Facsimile: (604) 822-6603
e-mail: cedwards@interchange.ubc.ca

CANADIAN CATALOGUING IN PUBLICATION DATA

Main entry under title:
    Critical challenges in English for secondary students

    (Critical challenges across the curriculum series, ISSN 1205-9730 ; v. 6)
    Co-published by: Field Relations and Teacher In-Service Education, Faculty of Education, Simon Fraser University.
    ISBN 0-86491-204-8

    1. English language—Study and teaching (Secondary) 2. Language arts (Secondary) I. Butler, Samantha, 1968- II. Husarski, Holly, 1970- III. Shea, Nancy, 1965- IV. Critical Thinking Cooperative. V. Simon Fraser University. Faculty of Education. Field Relations and Teacher In-Service Education. VI. Series.
LB1631.C74 1998   428'.0071'2   C98-910959-3

Contents

Foreword

Critical Challenges Across the Curriculum is an ongoing series of teacher resources focussed on infusing critical thinking into every school subject and at all levels. Two features distinguish this series from many other publications on critical thinking—our *curriculum embedded* approach and our emphasis on *teaching the intellectual tools*.

Our approach is to embed critical thinking by presenting focussed questions or tasks that invite critical student reflection about the content of the curriculum. We do not support the view of critical thinking as a set of generic skills or processes that can be developed independent of content and context. Nor do we believe that critical thinking can adequately be addressed as an add-on to the curriculum. Rather, if it is to take a central place in the classroom, critical thinking must be seen as a way of teaching the content of the curriculum. Teachers can help students understand the subject matter, as opposed to merely recall it, by providing continuing opportunities for thoughtful analysis of issues or problems that are central to the subject matter.

The second distinguishing feature of this series is our emphasis on systematically teaching the intellectual tools for critical thinking. Much of the frustration teachers experience when attempting to engage students in thinking critically stems from students' lack of the required concepts, attitudes, knowledge, criteria or strategies—in short, they lack the tools needed to do a competent job. It is often assumed that the mere provision of invitations to think will improve students' reflective competence. We believe that constructing a thoughtful response is like building a house in that it is impossible to do a competent job in either case unless one has the necessary tools. For this reason, each critical thinking challenge in the series includes a list of the tools needed to respond competently and, more importantly, activities suggesting how these tools may be taught.

We hope that teachers will find these resources of use in increasing and improving the teaching of critical thinking in their subject areas.

Roland Case & LeRoi Daniels

Series Editors

Preface and Acknowledgments

It is imperative that our students develop their ability to think critically—to formulate their own thoughtful opinions rather than to naively accept the ideas of others' at face value. This means that they must acquire the "tools" to think and communicate competently and intelligently. This collection of critical challenges introduces a range of key tools that secondary school students require for thinking about various genres of literature. In many cases the lessons are self-contained and can be taught as individual lessons; others must be part of a larger unit of study about a play or novel.

Most of the critical challenges in this collection were developed and piloted by secondary school teachers of the Okanagan Similkameen School District, British Columbia, between October 1996 and June 1997. Their names are listed as contributing authors to this resource. In addition to these teachers, we would like to thank the following educators for their help in this project:

Darlene Abbie	Okanagan Similkameen School District
Lindsay Abbie	Okanagan Similkameen School District
Phyllis Schwartz	Vancouver School District

Special thanks goes to Superintendent Brian Fox for his initiative to bring the TC^2 critical thinking model to our school district. Further thanks to Okanagan Similkameen School District for its leadership and ongoing financial support of this project.

Samantha Butler, Holly Husarski & Nancy Shea

Editors

Guide to the Lesson Format

Each of the critical challenges in this resource has the following components.

Early Renaissance art

Critical Challenge

Critical Task

Create an art form using symbols from the Renaissance period to portray some aspect of the present age.

Overview

Students are introduced to three aspects of symbolism—the symbol itself, the meaning behind the symbol and the explanation of the origins and meaning of the symbol. Through discussion of two Early Renaissance Flemish paintings about weddings—ones by Jan Van Eyck and Pieter Bruegel—aided by brief commentaries, students learn about the symbolism in use during this period. Students represent some aspect of the Renaissance using historically plausible symbols. They explain the symbolism in their own work and prepare a commentary on the symbolism in another student's work.

Requisite Tools

Background knowledge
- symbolism used by Renaissance artists
- information about Renaissance period

Criteria for judgment
- criteria for powerful symbolism (e.g., historically plausible, clarity, depth of meaning, sound justification)

Critical thinking vocabulary
- symbol and symbolism

Thinking strategies
- data comparison charts

Habits of mind
- attention to detail

---

*The **critical challenge** opens with a **critical question** or **critical task** that students will be asked to address.*

*An **overview** describes the focus of the lesson and the main activities that students will undertake.*

***Requisite tools** provides an inventory of the specific intellectual resources that students will need to use in competently addressing the critical challenge.*

Suggested activities

◆ Ask students to list five words that come to mind when they hear the word "witches" and to answer the questions "Is a witch-hunt a good thing? Why or why not?" Invite students to share their answers with the rest of the class. Look for patterns in their responses (e.g., witch-hunt is not taken seriously, witches are seen to deserve their punishment). If students have heard of the Inquisition or of Senator McCarthy's purge of American communists ask them to compare their reactions to these events to a witch-hunt. If their reactions are different, ask students to speculate about the reasons for this difference.

◆ Explain to students that during the 15th and 17th centuries in Europe it is estimated by historians that between 100,000 and 300,000 persons were killed and that more than double this number were imprisoned or banished because they were accused of witchcraft. Introduce the *Briefing Sheet: Witch-hunts during the Renaissance* (Blackline Master) and ask students to read the document on their own or aloud as a class.

Information about the witch-hunt

◆ Introduce the concepts of hypothesis and supporting evidence if students are not already familiar with these terms. Ask students to think about why the witch-hunts occurred at this time, and what evidence can they find to support their hypotheses.

hypothesis and supporting evidence

Evaluation

◆ Evaluate the *Data Chart* on the number of plausible hypotheses and on the amount and quality of evidence offered in support of each hypothesis.

◆ Evaluate responses to the critical challenge on the basis of ability to offer a plausible justification and sensitivity to the inadequate nature of the evidence to support a definitive justification of the "cause."

Extension

◆ Assign students to review their textbook for the period from the 15th to the 17th century and assess how much attention, if any, is paid to the witch-hunt. Ask students to consider that if the estimates of up to 300,000 deaths and 600,000 prosecutions are accurate, do they think that these episodes have been given adequate attention in the book. Assign students to make a list of the events that are included in their textbook for this period that in their eyes have less historical significance than the witch-hunt. Invite students to speculate why these events would be given greater attention than the witch-hunt.

---

*The body of the lesson is found under **suggested activities** which indicate how the critical challenge may be introduced and how the requisite tools may be taught. **Icons** in the side panel point out which specific tool is being addressed. Also provided in **evaluation** are assessment criteria and procedures, and in **extension** are found ideas for further exploration or broader application of key ideas found in the lesson.*

***References** are provided whenever published resources are referred to in the lesson plan.*

Who should we believe?

What features of the sources of information listed below would be relevant in determining the credibility of the three biographies of former Canadian Prime Minister, Brian Mulroney?

Jill Kin is Brian Mulroney's sister-in-law. She was given a high-paying job when Mulroney became Prime Minister. This is Jill's first published book. It is based on extensive personal conversations with Mulroney and with many other politicians over a ten-year period.

Features that enhance credibility	Features that diminish credibility

Phil Buster is a journalist with twenty-five years experience covering government affairs for the *Globe and Mail*. Phil was very critical of the Mulroney government, having exposed several instances of financial mismanagement and corruption. He has won several journalistic awards over the course of his career. The biography is based largely on public documents and personal observations—neither Mulroney or any of his supporters would talk to Phil.

Features that enhance credibility	Features that diminish credibility

Sally and Stephen Stage are two of Canada's most famous playwrights. They have written over twenty plays most of them taking a humorous look at famous people. Their latest stage play, *The Life of Brian*, is about the former Prime Minister. It is based entirely on the books by Jill Kin and Phil Buster. The Stages won an award as the best Canadian playwrights of the year.

Features that enhance credibility	Features that diminish credibility

Which source would be the most reliable? Why?

Which would be the least trustworthy? Why?

Student Activity
Page 1 of 1

Blackline masters *follow each lesson. These are the reproducible learning resources referred to in the suggested activities. There are six types of masters:*

- ***briefing sheets*** *provide background information to students;*

- ***data charts*** *contain various organizers for recording and analyzing information;*

- ***documents*** *refer to primary source material;*

- ***reproductions*** *include paintings and other illustrations;*

- ***student activities*** *provide questions and tasks for students to complete;*

- ***transparencies*** *refer to material that can be converted to a transparency for use on an overhead projector.*

Reading Source Materials

Source materials appear in many of these lessons and may present a challenge to students. Below are four strategies that may help students increase their abilities and confidence in understanding difficult reading material.

Decoding foreign text

Encourage students to read documents as if they were written in a foreign language and need to be translated. This approach may be introduced in the following manner:

1. Write the following sentence on the board:

    Today's homework has been _____ due to an_____ on your teacher's part to _____ the assignment at home.

    Ask students to offer guesses as to what the full sentence might say.

2. Insert the following sets of words in the blank spaces.

    Today's homework has been *(1) cancelled (2) delayed (3) increased* due to an *(1) error (2) unwillingness (3) urge* on your teacher's part to *(1) verify (2) mark (3) burn* the assignment at home.

    Invite students to read out the first, second and third possibilities for this sentence.

3. Point out how the meaning changes dramatically depending on which words are inserted. The objective is to help students appreciate how badly they can be misled if they do not understand all the *key* terms in a passage.

4. Discuss strategies for helping students decode unknown words. A list could be posted in the classroom that includes the following:

    *   guess at its meaning and confirm that this interpretation makes sense in light of the rest of the sentence or passage;

    *   as a clue to its meaning, check if the word resembles another word that is familiar (e.g., 'benefactor' is similar to 'benefit');

    *   look up the meaning in a dictionary or glossary;

    *   ask a fellow student or the teacher for help.

Team reading

Prepare students to work in teams to decode difficult passages by using the following suggested activity:

1. Organize students into teams of two or three.

2. Assign students to read the document and ask team members the meanings of words that they do not understand; if no one on the team can explain the meaning of an unknown word, use a dictionary or ask the teacher for a definition.

3. After all team members have completed their reading, direct students to tell other team members what they think is the basic idea of the document. Once agreement has been reached, the team tells the teacher their agreed upon answer.

4. Ask students to look again at the document closely, perusing the document for deeper meaning and identifying problematic areas; repeat the process of asking other team members or the teacher for clarification.

5. Finally, ask the team to prepare a précis that includes a two- or three- sentence summary of the essential meaning of the document, a theme statement and a conclusion.

SQ3R

The traditional SQ3R Method (survey, question, read, recall, review) provides a familiar procedure for some students; this method can be used in a group activity as outlined above or carried out as a class activity.

1. *Survey*: the teacher provides an overview of the topic addressed in the document.

2. *Question*: students pose questions that they have about the topic that may be addressed in the document before them.

3. *Read*: students read the document.

4. *Recall*: students share the main ideas of what they have just read.

5. *Review*: the teacher returns to the questions posed initially by students and discusses with the class any answers that may have been provided.

Graphic representation

Drawing can help students to visualize their reading; this method is used in *Ashoka's conversion to Buddhism* and is presented below as a model for this approach.

1. Assign students to read the document.

2. Ask students to sketch a picture of an image from the reading (or, in the case of longer passages, an assigned section) that they found particularly striking. Post their images in a collage grouping, providing students the opportunity to view the work of others.

3. Invite students to discuss in small groups what is contained in each picture and what it signifies.

Introduction to Critical Thinking

Understanding Critical Thinking

There are many conceptions or accounts of what is involved in thinking critically. The model described here is more fully explained in two articles in the *Journal of Curriculum Studies* entitled "Common Misconceptions of Critical Thinking" and "A Conception of Critical Thinking" by Sharon Bailin, Roland Case, Jerrold Coombs and LeRoi Daniels. For reasons explained below, we propose the following definition:

> *Critical thinking involves thinking through problematic situations about what to believe or how to act where the thinker makes reasoned judgments that embody the qualities of a competent thinker.*

A person is attempting to think critically when she thoughtfully seeks to judge what would be sensible or reasonable to believe or do in a given situation. The need to reach reasoned judgments may arise in countless kinds of problematic situations such as trying to understand a passage in a text, trying to improve an artistic performance, making effective use of a piece of equipment, or deciding how to act in a delicate social situation. What makes these situations problematic is that there is some doubt as to the most appropriate option.

Critical thinking is sometimes contrasted with problem solving, decision making, issue analysis and inquiry. We see these latter terms for rational deliberation as occasions for critical thinking. In all these situations, we need to think critically about the options. There is limited value in reaching solutions or making choices that are not sensible or reasonable. Thus, the term critical thinking draws attention to the quality of thinking required to competently pose and solve problems, reach sound decisions, identify and resolve issues, plan and conduct thoughtful inquiries and so on. In other words, thinking critically is a way of carrying out these thinking tasks just as being careful is a way of walking down the stairs. Thinking critically is not a unique *type* of thinking that is different from other types of thinking, rather it refers to the *quality* of thinking. The association of critical thinking with being negative or judgmental is misleading, since the reference to critical is to distinguish it from uncritical thinking—thinking that accepts conclusions at face value without any assessment of their merits or bases. It is more fruitful to interpret critical in the sense of critique—looking at the merits and shortcomings of alternatives in order to arrive at a reasoned judgment.

Our focus on the quality of thinking does not imply that students must arrive at a preconceived right answer, rather we look to see that their responses exhibit the qualities that characterize good thinking in a given situation. For example, students' responses to a request to cooperatively plan a field trip through group discussion may be judged in light of the accuracy and adequacy of information, how seriously students considered the ideas of others, willingness to express their own ideas, and respect for the ideas of those with whom they disagree. These are all qualities that a competent thinker would exhibit. Similarly, a critically thoughtful response to a newspaper editorial would likely include the following characteristics: sensitivity to any bias on the part of the writer, adequate consideration of alternative points of view, attention to the clarity of definition of key concepts, and assessment of evidence offered in support of the writer's position. We believe that emphasis on qualities that student responses should exhibit focuses teachers' attention on the crucial dimension in promoting and assessing students' competence in thinking critically. The challenge for teachers is to adopt practices that will effectively promote these qualities in their students.

Promoting Critical Thinking

To help students improve as critical thinkers, we propose a four-pronged approach:

- build a *community of thinkers* within the school and classroom;

- infuse opportunities for critical thinking—what we call *critical challenges*—throughout the curriculum;

- develop the *intellectual tools* that will enable students to become competent critical thinkers;

- on a continuing basis *assess students' competence* in using the intellectual tools to think through critical challenges.

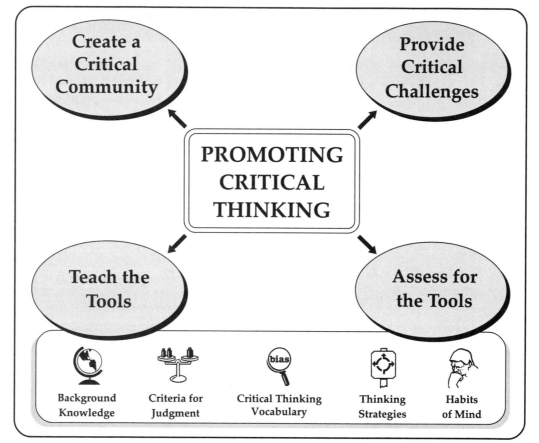

Building a community of thinkers

It is essential to infuse the expectations and opportunities to think critically throughout students' school lives. Developing supportive school and classroom communities where reflective inquiry is valued may be the most important factor in nurturing critical thinking. Many of the tools of critical thinking will not be mastered by students unless their use is reinforced on an ongoing basis. As well, the image of the thinker as a solitary figure is misleading. No one person can perfectly embody all the desired attributes—we must learn to rely on others to complement our own thoughts. Students will not learn how to be contributors to, and beneficiaries of, a community of thinkers unless they become members in that kind of community. There are many routines and norms that teachers can adopt to create this sense of community:

- As a matter of course, questions and assignments should have built-in expectations to think through, and not merely recall, what is being learned.

- Ongoing opportunities to engage in critical and cooperative dialogue—to confer, inquire, debate and critique—are key to creating a community of thinkers.

- Self- and peer-evaluation are excellent ways of involving students in thinking critically about their own work.

- Teacher modelling of good critical thinking practices is important. Students are more likely to learn to act in desired ways if they see teachers making every effort to be open-minded, to seek clarification where needed, to avoid reaching conclusions based on inadequate evidence, and so on. Opportunities to see their teachers as co-investigators, and not solely as resident experts, may send important messages to students about the need to think critically.

Infusing critical challenges throughout the curriculum

Critical thinking is always in response to a problematic situation, where judgment among alternatives is required. If students are to improve in their ability to think critically, they must have numerous opportunities to engage and think through problematic situations. We label as *critical challenges* those problematic situations which are deliberately presented to students for consideration.

Four questions should guide the choice of critical challenges.

- *Does the question or task require judgment?* Critical thinking occurs only in the context of a problematic situation. If an answer is simply there, waiting to be found, or if any and all answers are acceptable then there is no invitation to think critically. A question or task is a critical challenge only if it invites students to assess the reasonableness of plausible options or alternative conclusions; in short, the task must require more than retrieval of information, rote application of a strategy, uninformed guessing or mere assertion of a preference.

- *Will the challenge be meaningful to students?* We enhance our efforts to promote critical thinking if students find the questions interesting. Trivial, decontextualized mental exercises often alienate or bore students. It is important to frame challenges that are likely to engage students in tackling critical questions and tasks that they will find meaningful.

- *Does the challenge address key aspects of the subject matter?* If we are to make time for critical thinking the focus must be on matters that are at the heart of the curriculum—and not peripheral to it. As well, students are more likely to learn the content of the curriculum if they are invited to think critically about issues embedded in the subject matter.

- *Do students have the tools or can they reasonably acquire the tools needed to competently address the challenge?* Students are more likely to succeed if they possess the tools to deal with the challenge before them. Provision must be made to support students in acquiring the essential tools needed to competently meet the critical challenge. For this reason, challenges should be sufficiently focussed so that students are not overwhelmed by the enormity or complexity of the task.

Developing intellectual tools for thinking critically

The key to helping students develop as critical thinkers is to nurture competent use of five types of tools of thinking. These categories of tools are *background knowledge*, *criteria for judgment, critical thinking vocabulary, thinking strategies* and *habits of mind.*

Background Knowledge

—*the information about a topic required for thoughtful reflection*

Students cannot think deeply about a topic if they know little about it. Two questions to ask in developing this tool:
- What background information do students need for them to make a well-informed judgment on the matter before them?
- How can students be assisted in acquiring this information in a meaningful matter?

Criteria for Judgment

—*the considerations or grounds for deciding which of the alternatives is the most sensible or appropriate*

Critical thinking is essentially a matter of judging which alternative is sensible or reasonable. All judgments are based on criteria of some sort or other. Students need help in thinking carefully about the criteria to use when judging various alternatives.
- Is my estimate *accurate*?
- Is the interpretation *plausible?*
- Is the conclusion *fair* to all?
- Is my proposal *feasible*?

Critical Thinking Vocabulary

—*the range of concepts and distinctions that are helpful when thinking critically*

Students require the vocabulary or concepts that permit them to make important distinctions among the different issues and thinking tasks facing them. These include the following:
- inference and direct observation;
- generalization and over generalization;
- premise and conclusion;
- bias and point of view.

Thinking Strategies

—*the repertoire of heuristics, organizing devices, models and algorithms that may be useful when thinking through a critical thinking problem*

Although critical thinking is never simply a matter of following certain procedures or steps, numerous strategies are useful for guiding one's performance when thinking critically:
- *Making decisions:* Are there models or procedures to guide students through the factors they should consider (e.g., a framework for issue analysis or problem solving)?
- *Organizing information:* Would a graphic organizer (e.g., webbing diagrams, Venn diagrams, "pro and con" charts) be useful in representing what a student knows about the issue?
- *Role taking:* Before deciding on an action that affects others, should students put themselves in the others' positions and imagine their feelings?

Habits of Mind

—*the values and attitudes of a careful and conscientious thinker*

Being able to apply criteria and use strategies is of little value unless students also have the habits of mind of a thoughtful person. These include:
- *Open-minded:* Are students willing to consider evidence opposing their view and to revise their view should the evidence warrant it?
- *Fair-minded:* Are students willing to give impartial consideration to alternative points of view and not simply impose their preference?
- *Independent-minded:* Are students willing to stand up for their firmly held beliefs?
- *Inquiring or "critical" attitude:* Are students inclined to question the clarity of and support for claims and to seek justified beliefs and values?

Assessing for the tools

Assessment is an important complement to the teaching of the tools of critical thinking. As suggested by the familiar adages "What is counted counts" and "Testing drives the curriculum," evaluation has important implications for what students consider important and ultimately what students learn. Evaluations that focus exclusively on recall of information or never consider habits of mind fail to assess, and possibly discourage, student growth in critical reflection.

A key challenge in assessing critical thinking is deciding what to look for in a student's answer. If there is no single correct response, we may well ask: "On what basis, then, can we reliably assess students?" The qualities that we would expect to see exhibited in a successful response should provide the basis for our assessments. In the case of critical thinking, this means we would want to see whether or not students exhibited the qualities of a competent thinker. Thus, the intellectual resources or tools for critical thinking become the criteria for assessing students' work. More specifically, as students respond (orally, in writing, visually, etc.) to a critical challenge we should look for indications of the extent to which their comments or products reveal appropriate use of the desired tools. In other words, has the student:

- provided adequate and accurate information?
- satisfied relevant criteria for judgment?
- revealed understanding of important vocabulary?
- made effective use of appropriate thinking strategies?
- demonstrated the desired habits of mind?

The following example suggests each of the five types of critical thinking tools and specific assessment criteria that might be used in assessing evidence of critical thinking in an argumentative essay and an artistic work.

Type of criteria for assessment	Evidence of critical thinking in a persuasive essay	Evidence of critical thinking in an artistic work
Background Knowledge	• cited accurate information.	• revealed knowledge of the mechanics of the medium.
Criteria for Judgment	• provided ample evidence; • arranged arguments in logical sequence.	• work was imaginative; • work was clear and forceful.
Critical Thinking Vocabulary	• correctly distinguished "arguments" from "counter arguments."	• represented "point of view."
Thinking Strategies	• used appropriate strategies for persuasive writing.	• employed suitable rehearsal/preparation strategies.
Habits of Mind	• demonstrated an openness to alternative perspectives; • refrained from forming firm opinions where the evidence was inconclusive.	• was open to constructive criticism; • demonstrated a commitment to high quality; • demonstrated a willingness to take risks with the medium.

Peer- and self-assessment are especially effective means of encouraging critical thinking since the assessment of an assignment is a synonym for thinking critically about the assignment. The box below contains statements about several thinking strategies and habits of mind that students might consider as they self-assess their thoughtfulness as independent learners.

Self-assessment questions	Implied criteria for assessment
I thought about what I was expected to do before I started.	*Thinking Strategy:* before beginning, get clear about expectations
I asked for help whenever I needed it.	*Thinking Strategy:* ask for help
I stayed "on-task" until all my work was finished.	*Habit of Mind:* intellectual work ethic
I tried my best.	*Habit of Mind:* intellectual work ethic

Overview of Critical Challenges

Suggested grade level:

J = junior high   **S** = senior high school   **J/S** = both junior and senior high school

Novels		
Death by association	J	In the novel *The Outsiders* by S.E. Hinton, Johnny Cade is a character who suffers many injustices. Due to a series of unfortunate incidents, Johnny eventually dies. Students are shown how to diagram interdependent contributing factors to an event and then assigned to use the same strategy to assist them in determining which three characters are most responsible for Johnny's death.
Would the real Dallas please stand up?	J	Johnny describes Dallas as "gallant" on page 68 of *The Outsiders* by S.E. Hinton. Although Dallas is a juvenile delinquent, Johnny compares him to the confederate soldiers in the novel *Gone with the Wind*. Students define the word "gallant" and compile evidence from the novel to determine whether or not Dallas is gallant. Students draw inferences from Dallas' actions to determine if he can be called gallant and defend their position in a three-paragraph paper.
Who should we believe?	J	The novel *The Pigman* by Paul Zindel is written from two different teenager's points of view: John and Lorraine. As the point of view alternates from chapter to chapter the reader is left wondering which character is more credible. While their relationship with Mr. Pignati, an elderly man who befriends the two teens, is developing, both John and Lorraine go through feelings and experiences that will change them forever. Students complete a chart to analyze incidents reported on differently by both authors, review the text and identify criteria for establishing the credibility of an account. The challenge concludes with an individual written argument supporting the most reliable narrator in light of agreed-upon criteria.
Dumb blondes, stupid jocks and four eyed nerds	J	The novel *The Pigman* by Paul Zindel contains many examples of stereotyping. After reading the novel, students brainstorm and discuss several examples of stereotyping found in *The Pigman*. Students then look for stereotyping in their everyday world and the media. Finally, students work together to offer ways to dissolve stereotypes.
To be or not to be	J	The lesson begins with students exploring their pre-conceptions about seniors (or any other group). They then question whether or not their perceptions are based on stereotypes. Students learn to ask probing questions leading to the design of a questionnaire to uncover how teenagers are actually perceived by local senior citizens, what teenagers do to create these perceptions and what, if desired, they might do to improve them. Finally students redesign the questionnaire with an eye to making the questions more probing. As a by-product of preparing the questionnaire and analyzing the results students confront their own stereotypical assumptions about elderly people. This lesson links thematically with *The Pigman* by Paul Zindel and can be used as a follow-up to the critical challenge on stereotyping, "Dumb Blondes, Stupid Jocks and Four-Eyed Nerds."
Should it stay or go?	J/S	Every teacher has been faced with the question: "Why are we studying this novel?" This lesson attempts to work students through this question by asking them to generate criteria for selecting resource materials and then testing a book against these criteria. This lesson is developed in the context of *My Left Foot* by Christy Brown, which is most suitable for senior high students; however, the approach can be used with any novel at any grade level. The culminating activity is a letter to the Ministry of Education arguing for or against inclusion of the novel in the curriculum for their grade level.
Like a rolling stone	S	The novel *Lord of the Flies* by William Golding offers a scathing look at human nature and society. In the novel a physically unappealing character named Piggy is killed by a group of boys who have become uncivilized. After reviewing the legal terms of manslaughter, first degree murder and second degree murder, students decide whether or not to charge Jack, Ralph or Roger with a homicide offense.

Leader of the pack	S	This is the first of two challenges which use William Golding's novel, *Lord of the Flies* to deal with leadership. Students explore the attributes of good leaders and then match these against the qualities of two main characters in the novel, Ralph and Jack. Students discuss and eventually decide which of the two characters has the stronger leadership qualities.
Who said words can't kill you?	S	This is the second of two challenges about leadership using William Golding's novel *Lord of the Flies*. The characters who possess the best leadership qualities are not always the strongest leaders. This is also true with leaders in ordinary society. Often leaders find ways to become powerful to make up for their leadership deficiencies. In this lesson students examine the acquisition of power by using propaganda techniques. They examine the primary leaders in the novel, Ralph and Jack, and study how they use propaganda techniques to enhance their natural leadership skills. Students conclude their analysis of propaganda devices by writing about the most powerful leader in the novel.

Short Stories

A question of pride?	J	The protagonist Al Condraj must make a moral decision in the short story *The Parsley Garden*, by William Saroyan. The plot involves a young man from a low income, single parent family who shoplifts a hammer. He feels ashamed and humiliated by his action and, after working off his debt, he is faced with the decision to continue working and swallow his pride, or to continue on with his meager way of living, with his value system intact. Students make a judgment about Al's decision not to take a job. They then learn to think about counter-arguments as they re-evaluate their initial assessment of Al's decision.
Who done it?	J	In *The Moose and the Sparrow*, by Hugh Garner, the character Cecil is a slight young man who works at a logging camp during his summer breaks from University. Despite his pleasing personality and strong work ethic, Cecil is constantly being tormented by Moose Maddon—a man who is seemingly threatened by Cecil's intelligence. Moose has an unfortunate accident and the question is whether or not Moose's death was accidental. (There is speculation that perhaps Cecil is responsible.) Students must decide on the basis of evidence from the text whether or not the death was accidental. They then write an epilogue using evidence from the text to present their account of the death of Moose Maddon.
Daytime friends are night time lovers	S	The short story *The Painted Door* by Sinclair Ross is about a husband and wife who are facing difficulty in their marriage. Ann, the wife in the story, feels an attraction to her husband's friend Steven. As the story progresses Sinclair Ross is deliberately ambiguous about Ann's fidelity. Students first discuss what it means to be unfaithful and then examine Ann's fidelity or lack thereof. The culminating activity is to write two diary entries from Ann's point of view: one which points to her infidelity and the other which points to her fidelity. By doing this students also learn about counter argument. By doing this students also learn about counter-argument.

Poetry

Baseball is life . . . the rest is just details	J	The poem, *The Base Stealer*, by Robert Francis catches a crucial type of play in baseball. It can also be seen to describe many other things–life, decision making and growing up. Students read the poem with the title removed, hypothesize what it is about and then explore it as an extended metaphor.

Plays		
Back to the future	**J/S**	Many students question the relevance of studying Shakespeare. This challenge links themes found in Shakespearean plays to issues in modern society. Students evaluate the degree to which themes in *A Midsummer Night's Dream* are applicable to their own lives.
Dumb and dumber	**J**	The play *Romeo and Juliet* by William Shakespeare is a romantic tragedy that focuses on the lives of two teens as they meet and fall in love. They are victims of a long standing family feud preventing a relationship between these two lovers. This fate, combined with a series of events, leads to tragic deaths. Students examine the events leading to the deaths of Romeo and Juliet and argue to what degree these events were caused by fate (beyond their control) or by free will (the result of personal decisions).
"Quote, unquote"	**J/S**	This critical challenge can be used at any grade level with any piece of literature. This lesson focusses on Shakespeare's play *Macbeth*. Students explore the criteria for powerful and significant literary quotations and then search text looking for two quotes that satisfy these criteria. The class then judges the best among these quotes for inclusion in the culminating test for the unit.
The nobler character: Laertes or Hamlet?	**S**	Shakespeare frequently employed character foils in his plays. A foil can be defined as a character who, by contrast with the protagonist, underscores or enhances the distinctive characteristics of the protagonist. The focus in this critical challenge is on *Hamlet,* in particular Laertes (Ophelia's brother) and Hamlet. Students examine which of Laertes' circumstances are similar to those of Hamlet, and how the two characters react differently to similar circumstances. They consider the features of noble behaviour and then decide whether Hamlet or Laertes is portrayed as having the nobler character.

Essays		
Honesty: is it the best policy?	**S**	Andrea Chisholm's essay *The 'High' of an Honest Win* examines the question of cheating. Her thesis explores the the question of whether cheating is harmful to both the individual who cheats and the society to which he or she belongs. After a brief introduction to the topic of cheating, students will be asked to complete the Questionnaire on Cheating individually, and to complete two T-charts in small groups. Students will evaluate members of their group based on 'group work' criteria.

Songs		
Punctuating "Galileo"	**J/S**	The song *Galileo*, performed by the Indigo Girls and written entirely in lower case letters without punctuation, presents students with a unique punctuation task. These factors make the song difficult to follow on paper, therefore, it is a wonderful example of the importance of punctuation. Students listen to the song to hear punctuation clues, add the necessary punctuation marks to the text of the song lyrics and then rewrite the lyrics with punctuation corrections. Finally, students write an essay demonstrating their newfound knowledge about the importance of punctuation.

Fairy Tales		
On the other hand	**J/S**	Students are read a revised version of a classic fairy tale—possibly *The Frog Prince - Continued* (Jon Scieszka's remake of "The Frog Prince") or *The True Story of the Three Little Pigs by A. Wolf* (Jon Scieszka's remake of "The Three Little Pigs"). After discussing the notion of point of view and the techniques used to alter the point of view, students identify criteria of an effective "rewrite" of the fairy tale. Each student then selects a classic fairy tale and rewrites the story from a secondary character's point of view.

Death by association

Critical Challenge

Critical Question

Which three characters are most responsible for Johnny's death?

Overview

In the novel *The Outsiders* by S.E. Hinton, Johnny Cade is a character who suffers many injustices. Due to a series of unfortunate incidents, Johnny eventually dies. Students are shown how to diagram interdependent contributing factors to an event and then assigned to use the same strategy to assist them in determining which three characters are most responsible for Johnny's death.

Requisite Tools

Background knowledge
- familiarity with the novel *The Outsiders*

Criteria for judgment
- criteria for assigning responsibility (e.g., directly affected result, should have known better, acted freely)

Critical thinking vocabulary

Thinking strategies
- interdependent events diagram

Habits of mind

Suggested Activities

◆ To introduce the theme of interdependent events, begin with an example of a hypothetical but plausible local incident. The purpose of the exercise is to identify the groups/individuals who may have contributed (directly and indirectly) to this incident. It might be useful to provide the following scenario as an example:

A group of teens who like to skateboard have been kicked off a store's parking lot because of an increase in litter, and of vandalism to the store in the form of a large, elaborate skateboard symbol spray painted on the back of the building.

Using the *Transparency: Interdependent Events* (Blackline Master) as an overheard, or merely as a sample for creating your own diagram, walk students through a few of the factors that contributed to the incident. Start with the "Final Event" (e.g., teens being kicked off a parking lot) and identify the factors that contributed most directly to it, then trace the contributing factors to these direct factors.

interdependent events diagram

◆ Once the obvious individuals and contributing events have been plotted on the diagram, brainstorm suggestions for less obvious possibilities and record on a chart ways in which other individuals may have contributed to the turn of events. For the skateboard incident, the chart might look like the following:

Individuals involved	*Contribution to the incident*
parents	• lack of supervision • no established guidelines for dealing with right and wrong actions
community	• no provision of a skate park • no constructive activities for teens
local merchants	• allowed the teens to use their lot
teens	• making lots of noise and acting irresponsibly

◆ Organize students into small groups and assign them to finalize an interdependent events diagram for the hypothetical incident by plotting how all individuals identified in the above chart (and in the initial diagram) may have contributed to the final event. Encourage students to add to the list of individuals and contributing factors as they complete their diagram. Ask each group to consider which individuals should be considered most responsible for the final event and why they think so.

◆ After each group has had an opportunity to develop their own diagram, create a collective interdependent events diagram. Invite each group to contribute some aspect to the diagram. Encourage students to see the interdependence of events and the multiple factors that contribute to any single incident. Close the activity by discussing with the class which individuals are most responsible for the final incident.

◆ Connect this example to *The Outsiders* by asking students to list the names of all the characters in the novel who might have played a part in Johnny's death. Assign students to go back into the text to find quotes (noting page numbers) as evidence to support the hypothesis that this character was in some way responsible for Johnny's death.

familiarity with the novel

◆ Assign students to diagram this information on an interdependent events diagram—as they did for the skateboard incident—to indicate how members of the community may have contributed to the death of Johnny. Ask students to include quotes and page references on this diagram.

interdependent events diagram

◆ Organize students in pairs to compare and discuss their diagrams and, where needed, to refine and add to them.

◆ Explore with the class the basis for deciding upon degrees of responsibility. Invite students to consider various factors including the following:

criteria for assigning responsibility

   • Did the actions *directly affect the outcome*? (We are likely to diminish responsibility if there are many intervening events that need not have lead to the eventual outcome.)

   • Were the actions *deliberate and freely chosen*? (We often excuse those who had no choice in the matter—for example, if done in self-defense.)

   • Should the individual(s) *have known better*? (We are likely to hold a parent responsible for a young child causing damage with a dangerous object because we think that parents, but not young children, should know better than to allow children to come in contact with dangerous objects.)

◆ Present the critical question:

   Which three characters are most responsible for Johnny's death?

◆ Assign students to write a two-page essay naming the three characters and supporting, by detailed textual evidence, their view that these three characters deserve to be held most responsible for Johnny's death, given the previously-discussed criteria for assigning responsibility.

Evaluation

◆ Assess the interdependent events diagram according to the following criteria:

   • identification of how the actions of many of the characters in the novel may plausibly be seen to contribute to Johnny's death;

- clear indication of the interdependence and multiplicity of contributing factors.

◆ Assess the essays according to the following criteria:
- provide detailed evidence from the text in the form of direct quotes—at least one direct quote per character;
- explain how the actions of each of the three characters influenced Johnny's death—at least three actions per character;
- justify, in light of the criteria for assigning responsibility, why each character chosen was an important contributor to Johnny's death;
- use proper essay format, spelling and punctuation.

Extension

◆ Using peer evaluation, assign students to review one another's essays based on the evaluation criteria listed above.

◆ Adapt this lesson to analyze the cause of death in other works of literature such as *Romeo and Juliet, Macbeth* or *Julius Caesar*.

◆ Invite students to use the interdependent events diagram to plot the contributing factors of a topical event reported in the media.

Reference

Hinton, S.E. (1995). *The Outsiders*. New York: Dell Publishing. (ISBN 0-440-96769-4).

Interdependent events

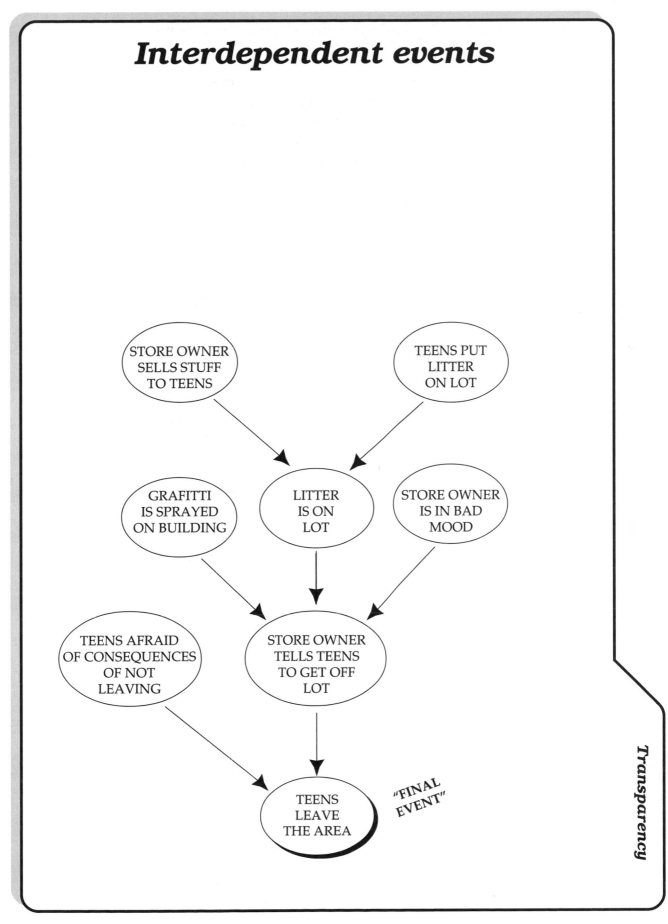

Transparency

Would the real Dallas please stand up?

Critical Challenge

Critical Question

Is Dallas gallant?

Overview

Johnny describes Dallas as "gallant" on page 68 of *The Outsiders* by S.E. Hinton. Although Dallas is a juvenile delinquent, Johnny compares him to the confederate soldiers in the novel *Gone with the Wind*. Students define the word "gallant" and compile evidence from the novel to determine whether or not Dallas is gallant. Students draw inferences from Dallas' actions to determine if he can be called gallant and defend their position in a three-paragraph paper.

Requisite Tools

Background knowledge	• familiarity with the novel *The Outsiders*.
	• definition of gallantry
Criteria for judgment	• consistent and plausible interpretation
Critical thinking vocabulary	• inference
Thinking strategies	• data chart
Habits of mind	

Suggested Activities

◆ This lesson is designed as a closing or consolidating activity after students have finished reading the novel *The Outsiders* by S.E. Hinton.

familiarity with the novel

◆ Define "gallant" for the students. You may wish to use the definition of gallant found in a dictionary: spirited, brave, noble, showy polite and attentive to women.

definition of gallant

◆ Ask students to compile a list of people they consider to be gallant, using the dictionary definition provided. At the junior high level it may be easier to begin this list by naming gallant people from the school and community before extending to a national or international scale.

◆ Once this list is compiled, ask students to provide examples of gallant actions for each individual on the list.

◆ Assign students to read the following passage from *The Outsiders* (page 68), which describes Dallas as a gallant character.

> "I bet they were cool ol' guys," he said, his eyes glowing after I had read the part about them riding into sure death because they were gallant. "They remind me of Dally."
>
> "Dally?" I said, startled, "Shoot, he ain't got any more manners than I do. And you saw how he treated those girls the other night. Soda's more like them Southern boys."
>
> "Yeah . . . in the manners bit, and the charm, too, I guess," Johnny said slowly, "but one night I saw Dally gettin' picked up by the fuzz, and he kept real cool and calm the whole time. They was gettin' him for breakin' out the windows in the school building, and it was Two-Bit who did that and Dally knew it. But he just took the sentence without battin' an eye or even denyin' it. That's gallant".
>
> That was the first time I realized the extent of Johnny's hero-worship for Dally Winston. Of all of us, Dally was the one I liked least. He didn't have Soda's understanding or dash, or Two-Bit's humor, or even Darry's superman qualities. But I realized that these three appealed to me because they were like the heroes in he novels I read. Dally was real. I liked my books and clouds and sunsets. Dally was so real he scared me.

◆ Ask students to identify Dallas' actions, Johnny's interpretation of them and Ponyboy's interpretation of them. It might be helpful to diagram this information for the students as follows:

inference

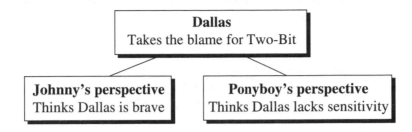

```
                    ┌─────────────────────────┐
                    │        Dallas           │
                    │ Takes the blame for Two-Bit │
                    └─────────────────────────┘
                        /              \
    ┌──────────────────────┐    ┌──────────────────────┐
    │ Johnny's perspective │    │ Ponyboy's perspective │
    │ Thinks Dallas is brave│    │Thinks Dallas lacks sensitivity│
    └──────────────────────┘    └──────────────────────┘
```

◆ Define and introduce the concept of inference. Ask students to write down other interpretations of Dallas' action (taking the blame for Two-Bit). It might be helpful to offer examples to begin this activity:

> Dallas wants Two-Bit to like him.

> Dallas wanted to be blamed for the vandalism.

◆ Compile a class list of inferences and discuss which of these inferences is the most plausible in light of Dallas' other actions in the novel. Once class consensus is reached and students have a good grasp of the concept of a plausible inference, assign students to work in pairs to complete *Data Chart: Is Dallas Gallant?* (Blackline Master).

data chart

◆ Once the data are collected, assign students to discuss which inference(s) is (are) most consistent with the rest of the text and identify on the Data Chart that or those inference(s) using a highlighter pen.

consistent and plausible interpretation

◆ When this task is completed, ask students to report their decisions in a class discussion and conclude by discussing with the class Dallas' character traits. After some discussion present the critical question:

> Is Dallas gallant?

◆ Assign students to write a three-paragraph statement that argues whether or not Dallas is gallant using evidence from both the Data Chart and the class discussion.

Evaluation

◆ Evaluate the Data Chart on the number of relevant statements and actions that students identify and on their ability to offer at least two plausible inferences for each selection from the text.

◆ Evaluate the three-paragraph statement on student's ability to use information in the story to provide a consistent and plausible interpretation of Dallas' gallantry and on their understanding of the definition of the word 'gallant.'

Extension

◆ Assign students to write on the following topics:
- Is gallantry dead today?
- Should gallantry survive as a desirable character trait?

Resource

Hinton, S.E. (1995). *The Outsiders*. New York: Bantam Doubleday Dell Publishing. (ISBN: 0-440-96769-4).

Is Dallas gallant?

DALLAS' WORDS	PAGE	WHAT IT TELLS US ABOUT HIM	OTHER INFERENCES
1. "I'm never nice"	22	Appears "tough"	low self-esteem
2.			
3.			
4.			
5.			
6.			
7.			
8.			
9.			
10.			
DALLAS' ACTIONS	PAGE	WHAT IT TELLS US ABOUT HIM	OTHER INFERENCES
1. Gives the boys money	55	Shows he cares for his friends	Wants others to like him
2.			
3.			
4.			
5.			
6.			
7.			
8.			
9.			
10.			

Data Chart

Who should we believe?

Critical Challenge

Critical Question

Who provides a more believable picture of events in *The Pigman*, John or Lorraine?

Overview

The novel *The Pigman* by Paul Zindel is written from two different teenager's points of view: John and Lorraine. As the point of view alternates from chapter to chapter the reader is left wondering which character is more credible. While their relationship with Mr. Pignati, an elderly man who befriends the two teens, is developing, both John and Lorraine go through feelings and experiences that will change them forever. Students complete a chart to analyze incidents reported on differently by both authors, review the text and identify criteria for establishing the credibility of an account. The challenge concludes with an individual written argument supporting the most reliable narrator in light of agreed-upon criteria.

Requisite Tools

Background Knowledge	• familiarity with the novel *The Pigman*
Criteria for judgment	• criteria for believability (e.g., consistency of information, plausibility of statement, credibility of character)
Critical thinking vocabulary	• point of view • corroborating evidence
Thinking strategies	
Habits of mind	

Suggested Activities

◆ Show students two newspaper articles or letters to the editor written from two different points of view and discuss the discrepancies between the two. These articles may be selected from different newspapers or differing letters to the editor on the same issue.

point of view

◆ Assign students to work in partners to formulate and write a definition of point of view. Share definitions in class discussion and work toward a class definition of point of view.

◆ Discuss a school event that could be seen from different points of view (for example, an incident that occurred in the cafeteria during lunch time as seen by the group of students involved, uninvolved observers and the teachers or administrators supervising the cafeteria). Ask students to write about the incident from each point of view, read some of these descriptions to the class and discuss the differences among the different points of view.

◆ If students have not already read the novel, *The Pigman,* assign this task. Introduce the differences between John's and Lorraine's points of view. Remind students that the reader does not know for a fact that what each character reports is true or accurate. Ask students to think about which of the two narrators offers the more credible version of the story.

familiarity with the novel

◆ Assign students to complete *Student Activity: What Actually Happened?* (Blackline Master). Introduce the following criteria for assessing the credibility of an account and work through an example on the chart before students begin this assignment individually or in pairs:

criteria for believability

  • Is the account consistent with other information in the story?

  • Is it plausible that things could have happened as stated?

  • Does one character seem more credible than the other?

◆ After completing the sheet, discuss the results of the student activity sheet. Encourage students to corroborate their accounts with evidence from the text. Explain that corroborating evidence is one or more statements (observations, etc.) that backs up or reinforces another statement. In a court of law, for example, accused persons are asked to supply corroborating evidence which supports their account of what happened.

corroborating evidence

◆ Present the critical question:

  Who provides a more believable picture of events in *The Pigman,* John or Lorraine?

Suggest that students write a short paper (approximately one page in length) that answers the question. Share with students the criteria upon which their papers will be assessed.

Evaluation

◆ Assess the Student Activity sheet on the following criteria:
- accurately and clearly identifies John's and Lorraine's account of each incident;
- identifies relevant information from the text to corroborate or contradict each account;
- offers a plausible account of what actually happened, given the evidence.

◆ Assess the short paper on the following criteria:
- clearly expresses their position and reasons;
- offers ample relevant evidence to support their position;
- work is technically proficient—complete sentences, cohesive paragraphs, etc.

Extension

◆ Write an incident from the story through another point of view; for example, write about the party at Mr. Pignati's house from the policeman's point of view.

Reference

Zindel, Paul. (1983). *The Pigman*. New York: Bantam Books. (ISBN 0-553-23540-0).

What actually happened?

As you look for evidence in the text to corroborate John or Lorranie's account of each incident, look for *consistency* with other parts of the book, *plausibility* of statements, and signs of who is the more *credible character*. Finally, offer what you think actually happened for each incident.

Incident	John's statement about the incident	Lorraine's statement about the incident	Corroborating evidence from the text	Your version of what actually happened

Student Activity

Dumb blondes, stupid jocks and four-eyed nerds

Critical Challenge

Critical Task

Create a poster which 'tears down' a stereotype for your assigned group.

Overview

The novel *The Pigman* by Paul Zindel contains many examples of stereotyping. After reading the novel, students brainstorm and discuss several examples of stereotyping found in *The Pigman*. Students then look for stereotyping in their everyday world and the media. Finally, students work together to offer ways to dissolve stereotypes.

Requisite Tools

Background knowledge	• familiarity with the novel *The Pigman* • knowledge of anti-stereotyping strategies
Criteria for judgment	• features of an effective anti-stereotyping poster (e.g., presents a full portrait, has powerful impact, fairly represents the subject or group)
Critical thinking vocabulary	• stereotype
Thinking strategies	• role-play • data chart
Habits of mind	

Suggested Activities

◆ Define the term "stereotype" using the following types of stereotyping as a guideline:

1. an unfair account of an *individual* where we see only a narrow range of things about a person instead of the full picture. It is a stereotype because our perception fails to recognize the multiple features or attributes of an individual

stereotype

(e.g., focusing on the differences in their speech or skin colour but overlooking a range of other ways in which they are very similar to us; or focussing on the times a person is grumpy while overlooking her sense of humour and wilingness to help others);

2. an unfair account of a *group* where we overgeneralize the actions or features of a few members of that group. It is a stereotype because our perception fails to recognize the diversity within the group, that all in the group are not a particular way (e.g., not all women are "soft," and not all convicts are mean).

◆ To dramatize the fact that we often see things from different perspectives, organize students into groups to role-play the following scenario for the class from a variety of points of view based on perceived perceptions.

role-play

> *The scenario:* City planners building a skateboard park on a vacant lot in a residential area.

> *Role-play characters:* police officer, parent, an elderly person, a teenager, a contractor, a neighbour on the block where the park will be built, a manufacturer of skateboards.

◆ Assign each group to write out their role-play script and provide instructions to capture tone of voice, facial expressions characteristic of this interest group; for example: anger, frustration, happiness, apprehension.

◆ After each presentation, debrief each scenario in a class discussion, considering the following questions as guidelines:

• What assumptions were made about how people would feel and act? Why?

• Do all people in a particular group fit the stereotype presented?

• Why do we feel the need to group, label or generalize about people?

◆ Assign students as a homework assignment to examine two television shows and two magazines to observe stereotyping using *Data Chart: #1 Media Stereotyping* (Blackline Master). Direct students to focus on the portrayal of minority groups, people of colour, senior citizens and teens.

data chart

◆ As a class, discuss the results of their observations. Elicit student feelings about the stereotypes, particularly those of teens.

◆ Organize students into groups and assign a commonly held stereotyped group for analysis and strategies for overcoming the stereotypes. Use the following list as a start: ethnic group, religious group, parents, teachers, teenagers, skaters, politicians, police officers, homeless people, senior citizens. It may be useful to provide positive examples of anti-stereotyping found in the media. For example, Benetton clothing ads include a cross section of cultures, or men shown in primary care giver roles in the home.

◆ Using *Data Chart #2: Combatting Stereotypes* (Blackline Master) to focus their thinking, ask each group to brainstorm three or four techniques for overcoming each of four ways in which their particular group is stereotyped. It might be useful to provide an example such as the following:

data chart

Target group: Teenagers

Stereotype: all teenagers shoplift (teens are greeted as they enter a store and followed until they make a purchase or leave the store)

Strategies for overcoming the stereotype:
1. make eye-contact with merchant
2. greet them with a smile
3. ask for help
4. provide honest answers when employees ask if you need help.

◆ Follow this group activity with a brief group report and class discussion to evaluate strategies for overcoming stereotyping.

◆ Assign students to revisit the original copy of their stereotyping role-play and re-examine it in light of what they have learned about stereotyping by answering the following questions.

knowledge of anti-stereotyping strategies

• Is the character portrayed as a stereotype?

• To what degree is it a fair or unfair portrait?

• What part of your role-play will you change?

• How will you do this?

◆ Ask students to rewrite their original script to their role-play reflecting techniques learned by analyzing and brainstorming strategies for overcoming stereotyping.

◆ Direct groups to exchange both their original and adapted versions of their role-play scripts for peer evaluation with another group. Ask groups members to provide feedback on the degree to which the adapted copy is free from stereotyping. It is important to allow sufficient discussion time for this activity so that students can add further suggestions about how to reduce stereotyped portraits in their role-play scripts.

◆ Present the critical task:

> Create a poster which 'tears down' a stererotype for your assigned group.

◆ Discuss with students criteria for an effective anti-stereo-typing poster. As a class make a list of the key features they should aim for in designing their poster (e.g., presents full portrait of the group, has a powerful impact on the audience, fairly represents information).

features of effective anti-stereotyping posters

It may help students to begin with a profile of the stereotypes which exist for the particular group that is the subject of their poster. They may also find it helpful to interview members of this group of people to obtain a comprehensive image of them. It might also be beneficial for students to collect a variety of images found in magazines or other visual sources.

Evaluation

◆ Evaluate *Data Chart #2: Combatting Stereotypes* on students' ability to identfiy at least four common stereotypes of their target group and on their ability to generate three or four effective strategies to address each stereotype.

◆ Assess the revised non-stereotyping script on the fullness and diversity of the description of characters.

◆ Evaluate the poster on how well they satisfy the agreed-upon criteria of an effective poster.

Extension

◆ Write a letter to a particular company or TV show suggesting how they could overcome stereotypical representation in their product ads. Mail the letters to the respective companies and wait for a response!

◆ Follow this lesson with the critical challenge, "To Be or Not To Be," dealing with the stereotyping betwen teenagers and seniors.

◆ Apply the activities in this lesson to other works of literature in which stereotyping is evident; for example, the short story "Charles" by Shirley Jackson.

Reference

Zindel, Paul. (1983). *The Pigman*. New York: Bantam Books. (ISBN 0-553-23540-0).

Media stereotyping

	TELEVISION		
Program	**Example(s) of stereotyping**	**Source: program or ad**	**Time of day**
Friends	*Phoebe is the only blonde primary character and is portrayed as scattered and lacking seriousness. She is set up as a "dumb blonde" stereotype*	*program*	*8:00 pm*

Data Chart #1
page 1 of 2

MAGAZINES		
Title of Magazine	**Advertisement**	**Example of Stereotyping**
Cosmopolitan	Calvin Klein	An extremely under-the-average-weight Kate Moss models for Calvin Klein. This stereotype at work is that, to look good, women must be unnaturally lean

Combatting stereo types

Target group _____

Stereotype	Strategies for combatting stereotype
	1. 2. 3. 4.
	1. 2. 3. 4.
	1. 2. 3. 4.
	1. 2. 3. 4.

Data Chart #2

To be or not to be

Critical Challenge

Critical Task

Design a revised questionnaire, using a set of probing questions, to delve into seniors' attitudes towards teenagers.

Overview

The lesson begins with students exploring their pre-conceptions about seniors (or any other group). They then question whether or not their perceptions are based on stereotypes. Students learn to ask probing questions leading to the design of a questionnaire to uncover how teenagers are actually perceived by local senior citizens, what teenagers do to create these perceptions and what, if desired, they might do to improve them. Finally students redesign the questionnaire with an eye to making the questions more probing. As a by-product of preparing the questionnaire and analyzing the results students confront their own stereotypical assumptions about elderly people. This lesson links thematically with *The Pigman* by Paul Zindel and can be used as a follow-up to the critical challenge on stereotyping, "Dumb Blondes, Stupid Jocks and Four-Eyed Nerds."

Requisite Tools

Background knowledge	• knowledge of seniors' attitudes towards teenagers
Criteria for judgment	• criteria of a probing question
Critical thinking vocabulary	• stereotype
Thinking strategies	
Habits of mind	

Suggested Activities

◆ This challenge focusses on senior citizens, but can be used with any group from the local community who you know is often stereotyped by teenagers. Distribute *Student Activity #1: Thinking about Seniors* (Blackline Master) and ask students individually to write in the column titled "First Thoughts" their answers to following questions:

• What is your attitude toward seniors?

• What is their attitude toward you?

• What behaviour do you display when you are around seniors?

• How do you feel when seniors generalize about teenagers?

◆ Write the phrase "senior citizens" (or another group's name) on the board and, without explanation, have students list on a piece of paper any associations they have regarding this group. Ask students to share their ideas in an open class session. Record students' ideas on the board in a web around the phrase 'senior citizen'. (If the discussion is slow to get started, ask students what they think seniors' attitudes toward teenagers are.)

◆ In reference to the ideas about seniors recorded on the board, ask the class "Why do we believe these to be true?" Compile students' responses by having them write their answers on a second section of the board.

◆ Define the term 'stereotype' or review the definition of stereotype from the critical challenge, "Dumb Blondes, Stupid Jocks and Four Eyed Nerds." It may be useful to discuss two types of stereotype:

stereotype

1. an unfair account of an *individual* where we see only a narrow range of things about a person instead of the full picture. It is a stereotype because our perception fails to recognize the multiple features or attributes of an individual (e.g., focussing on the differences in their speech or skin colour but overlooking a range of other ways in which they are very similar to us; or focussing on the times a person is grumpy while overlooking her sense of humour and willingness to help others);

2. an unfair account of a *group* where we overgeneralize the actions or features of a few members of that group. It is a stereotype because our perception fails to recognize the diversity within the group, that all in the group are not a particular way (e.g., not all women are "soft", and not all convicts are mean).

◆ On a third section of the board, record students' responses to the following questions:

- Are all seniors actually like this or are these stereotypes?

- What information would we need to confirm our views?

As a class, reflect on the ideas recorded on the board and identify those which may be based on stereotypes.

◆ Ask students to revisit their answers in the "First Thoughts" column of *Student Activity #1* and highlight any stereotypical statements. In the "Second Thoughts" column, students should explain *why* these highlighted comments are stereotypical. Assign students into small groups (3-5 students each) to assess each person's work, checking whether or not the individual has correctly recognized and adequately explained his/her stereotypes.

◆ Suggest to students that the class find out exactly what perceptions seniors have of teenagers. Discuss creating a questionnaire. Explain that in order to do this students must generate thoughtful, probing question—questions that are effective at getting to the root of the issue. Invite students to offer criteria for a good probing question. Below are suggestions that students might consider if they are stuck for ideas of their own:

A probing question . . .

- is clearly worded;

- is open-ended (as opposed to closed-ended);

- is respectful of the person responding;

- makes no accusations or unfounded assumptions;

- seeks specific information.

criteria for probing question

◆ Provide students with a few examples of flawed questions (e.g., Why do you guys hastle us so often? What is your problem?) and ask students to apply the criteria to these questions—in so doing confirm that each student understands what is implied by the criteria and that the list of criteria they have developed is adequate. Agree on a list of criteria for a thoughtful, probing question and post this list in a prominent place in the classroom.

◆ Invite each student to write down two probing questions he or she would like to ask of senior citizens to uncover their attitudes toward teenagers. Remind students to produce questions which meet their criteria for probing questions.

◆ Arrange students in small groups to share and evaluate their questions in light of the agreed-upon criteria. If warranted, students should revise their questions so that they better meet the criteria. Instruct each to write their recommended set of questions on an overhead . (Limit to 10 the number of questions each group is to submit for review by the entire class.)

◆ Using an overhead projector, consider as a class each group's questions and evaluate them in light of the criteria. If questions are redundant or overlap, choose the better question or consolidate the questions. Record on the board the emerging list of recommended questions.

◆ Ask students working in small groups to rank order the questions according to effectiveness in serving the purpose of the questionnaire, which is to find out what seniors actually think about teenagers and why they think as they do. As a class decide on a suitable number of questions, perhaps from 7 to 12 questions in total.

◆ Create a rough draft of the questionnaire and distribute it for final review by students. Add or delete questions as students see fit and prepare the final copy of the questionnaire. See *Sample: Information Survey* for an actual questionnaire developed by a grade 9 class.

◆ Distribute the final questionnaire to a sampling of approximately 20 senior citizens, either by contacting a local senior's centre or by having students approach seniors they know to distribute the questionnaire to fellow seniors. Arrange for the completed questionnaires to be returned directly to the school as soon as possible.

◆ When a sufficient number of completed questionnaires have been returned, make copies for each group of 3-5 students. Students are to review the completed questionnaires for two purposes: initially, to learn more about how seniors actually feel about teenagers and, subsequently, to use the responses from the completed questionnaires to improve the questions asked on the questionnaire.

seniors' attitudes towards teenagers

◆ In their small groups students should read over the questionnaire responses before discussing the following questions:

  • What were you surprised to learn about senior's perceptions?

  • Were any of your preconceptions about the views of seniors unfounded?

  • What have you learned about your role/place in this community and in society more generally?

  • What have you learned about stereotyping others and about how to avoid being stereotyped yourself?

In a class discussion, invite students to share their reactions to the seniors' responses. Focus students' attention on the stereotypes that they may have held toward seniors.

◆ Ask students individually to again revisit *Student Activity #1: Thinking about Seniors* and complete the column "Third Thoughts" by reviewing what they had written in the other two columns and had heard in the class discussions. Students should write any final thoughts or comments about how their thinking has changed or deepened.

◆ Use any confusion or uncertainty arising from students' interpretations of questionnaire responses to raise the possibility of obtaining more and better information from seniors: "Could we have developed a more probing set of questions?" Present the critical task:

> Design a revised questionnaire, using a set of powerful questions, to delve into seniors' attitudes toward teenagers.

Ask students to create their own revised questionnaire. It may be helpful to provide students with a response format such as the one outlined in *Student Activity #2: Improving the Questionnaire* (Blackline Master). Students are to revise the original questionnaire based on the responses received. Suggest that students ask themselves the following questions as they think about each question:

• Do the responses match the intention of the question?

• How might it be improved (i.e., be made more probing)?

• Should the question be deleted?

• What additional question, if any, would be useful to ask?

Students may wish to revise or add to the previously developed list of criteria for probing questions.

Evaluation

◆ Assess the two questions posed initially by each student on how well they meet each of the agreed-upon criteria of a probing question (e.g., clear and concise, open ended, respectful, seek specific information).

◆ Assess the revised questionnaires on the basis of students' ability to improve the quality of the questions and to justify their recommended changes in light of the identified criteria of a probing question.

Extension

◆ A recurring theme in this critical challenge is the differences that occur when we revisit initial ideas after gathering additional information. What differences have students noticed in the before and after? Do they find this process of revisiting useful? worth the effort?

◆ Suggest that students send out their revised questionnaires to a new group of seniors to see what additional insights they can gain about seniors' attitudes towards teenagers.

◆ Invite students to decide upon and implement a strategy (or set of strategies) to improve perceptions between seniors and teenagers. (This activity ties in with the critical challenge "Dumb Blondes, Stupid Jocks and Four-Eyed Nerds".)

Reference

Zindel, Paul. (1983). *The Pigman.* New York: Bantam Books. (ISBN 0-553-23540-0)

Thinking about seniors

FIRST THOUGHTS	SECOND THOUGHTS	FINAL THOUGHTS
What is your attitude toward seniors?		
What is their attitude toward you?		
What behaviour do you display when you are around seniors?		
How do you feel when you hear seniors generalizing about teenagers?		

Student Activity #1

Information survey

The students of Ms. Shea's English 9 class are studying a novel that deals with the relationship between two teenagers and an older man. They have put together the following survey in the hopes of gaining a better understanding of how they are perceived by seniors in our community and what they do to promote these perceptions.

Please answer each question as fully as possible. Be honest!

1. How do you feel when other people criticize teenagers? Do you tend to join in or defend the teens? Why?

2. What is the first thought that comes into your mind when you see a group of teenagers? What makes you think this?

3. What do you think teens should do to be seen better in the eyes of the community?

4. What would you like to know about teenagers and their lifestyle?

5. What do you think about teenagers appearances? (dress, hair styles, etc.)

6. Do you think that you have ever prejudged teenagers based on stereotypes? Explain your reasoning.

7. Explain how you feel about the actions of teenagers in general. How do these actions affect you?

8. Why do you think some people have a negative attitude towards teens today?

9. How is a teenager today different from when you were a teenager?

10. What would you change about teenagers today if you had the power to do so?

11. If a rock hit your window and broke it and you looked outside and saw a neatly dressed teen and a teen wearing baggy clothes, who would you be more likely to suspect and why?

Sample

Example of a questionnaire prepared by Nancy Shea's grade 9 English class at Southern Okanagan Secondary in Oliver, B.C.

Improving the questionnaire

Instructions: You have been asked to suggest how the class-designed questionnaire could be improved. In the column on the left, beneath each of the original questions asked on our questionnaire, indicate what improvements, if any, (including replacing the question completely) you would recommend. In the column on the right justify each of your suggestions by explaining how your changes make the question more powerful.

QUESTION	REASON FOR CHANGE
Original question: 1. *Suggested revision:*	
Original question: 2. *Suggested revision:*	
Original question: 3. *Suggested revision:*	
Original question: 4. *Suggested revision:*	

QUESTION	REASON FOR CHANGE
Original question: 5. Suggested revision:	
Original question: 6. Suggested revision:	
Original question: 7. Suggested revision:	
Original question: 8. Suggested revision:	
Original question: 9. Suggested revision:	
Original question: 10. Suggested revision:	

Should it stay or go?

Critical Challenge

Critical Task

Write a letter to the provincial Ministry of Education arguing for the inclusion of *My Left Foot* (or some other novel) in the curriculum.

Overview

Every teacher has been faced with the question: "Why are we studying this novel?" This lesson attempts to work students through this question by asking them to generate criteria for selecting resource materials and then testing a book against these criteria. This lesson is developed in the context of *My Left Foot* by Christy Brown, which is most suitable for senior high students; however, the approach can be used with any novel at any grade level. The culminating activity is a letter to the Ministry of Education arguing for or against inclusion of the novel in the curriculum for their grade level.

Requisite Tools

Background knowledge	• familiarity with *My Left Foot*
Criteria for judgment	• qualities of an appropriate novel for use in school (e.g., interest to audience, rich use of language, universal message, appropriateness to audience) • qualities of a well written formal letter
Critical thinking vocabulary	
Thinking strategies	• data chart
Habits of mind	

Suggested Activities

◆ As part of the closing activities after a short story or novel study (in this case, Christy Brown's *My Left Foot*), students will develop arguments in defense of its place in the provincial curriculum. Introduce the lesson by asking students the following questions and recording their responses on the board:

• What is your favourite book/story you've read for school?

• What is your favourite "all time" book/story?

familiarity with the novel

◆ Once students have collectively made a list of favourite books organize students into small groups to compile a list of attributes of a good book. This is best be done on chart paper so that the lists can be displayed for comparison among groups.

qualities of an appropriate novel

After all groups' charts have been displayed, discuss the common criteria of a good book and reduce this list to approximately five criteria. Some criteria may include:

• interest to audience;

• rich use of language;

• universality (an important message with broad appeal).

Explain to students the curriculum resource selection in the province with a specific focus on the criteria which students believe ought to be established by the Ministry of Education for including a book in the curriculum. It may be valuable to present some of the social considerations such as gender equity, political or ethnic biases, portrayal of violence and language use. Encourage students to re-assess their criteria for a good book in light of the considerations that ought to govern provincial selection of reading materials.

◆ Distribute and assign students groups to complete *Student Activity: Curriculum Selection* (Blackline Master). It may be helpful to begin this activity as a class, completing the first criterion as follows:

data chart

Key features of a good novel	Looks like? Sounds like?	Example from novel
Interesting to audience very weak fair satisfactory good excellent 1 2 (3 3.5 4) 5	Looks like a book you can't put down	Pregnant mom falls down stairs while caring for her disabled son; disabled son has to get help for the mom

Critical Challenges Across the Curriculum

◆ After groups have evaluated the novel, organize a class discussion to determine whether or not this novel should be placed on the provincial curriculum. Coach students to develop arguments for or against its inclusion. Require that students make explicit references to the criteria for selection they are relying upon when offering reasons for their position.

◆ Once students are confident in their arguments and have generated sufficient criteria to support their positions, introduce the letter writing assignment and discuss the importance of audience when writing and developing arguments.

*qualities of a
formal letter*

◆ Present the critical task:

Write a letter to the provincial Ministry of Education arguing for the inclusion of *My Left Foot* (or some other novel) in the curriculum.

◆ Use *Transparency: Formal Letter Template* (Blackline Master) to provide the format of a formal business letter on the overhead projector. Discuss the following evaluation criteria to assist students in drafting this letter:

• clear explanation of criteria used for judging curriculum selection;

• appropriate, specific examples from the novel to support the conclusion reached;

• polite tone;

• error-free (i.e., spelling, grammar and style).

Evaluation

◆ Use the *Assessment Sheet: Formal Letter Evaluation* (Blackline Master) to involve students in peer and self assesment prior to submitting a final draft of their letter for teacher evaluation.

◆ Evaluate group work on effort and initiative taken to complete task and thoroughness of the completed chart work.

Extension

◆ Obtain a copy of the provincial resources selection criteria from the Ministry of Education and ask students to compare their criteria to the provincially-approved criteria.

Reference

Brown, Christy. (1995). *My Left Foot*. London: Mandarin Paperbacks. (ISBN 0 7493 9177 4).

Curriculum selection

Key features of a good novel	Looks like? Sounds like?	Examples from text
Interesting to audience very poor fair satisfactory good excellent 1 2 3 4 5		
Rich use of language very poor fair satisfactory good excellent 1 2 3 4 5		
Important universal message very poor fair satisfactory good excellent 1 2 3 4 5		
Appropriateness to general audience/age of audience very poor fair satisfactory good excellent 1 2 3 4 5		
    very poor fair satisfactory good excellent 1 2 3 4 5		
    very poor fair satisfactory good excellent 1 2 3 4 5		

Student Activity

Formal letter template

[your address - header on top of page]

Date

Name & address
of person
receiving letter

Dear _____:

Introductory paragraph (introduce yourself, purpose of letter)

Body (present arguments and provide examples)

Concluding paragraph (call for action, thank-you)

Salutation (Respectfully, Yours truly, Sincerely,)

[hand written signature]

Your name type-written

Transparency

Formal letter evaluation

	very poor 1	fair 2	satisfactory 3	good 4	excellent 5

Criteria	Self evaluation	Peer evaluation	Teacher evaluation
Clear explanation of criteria for judging curriculum selection	1 2 3 4 5 Explanation:	1 2 3 4 5 Explanation:	1 2 3 4 5 Explanation:
Appropriate, specific examples which support points made	1 2 3 4 5 Explanation:	1 2 3 4 5 Explanation:	1 2 3 4 5 Explanation:
Error free (i.e., spelling, grammar or style)	1 2 3 4 5 Explanation:	1 2 3 4 5 Explanation:	1 2 3 4 5 Explanation:
Polite tone	1 2 3 4 5 Explanation:	1 2 3 4 5 Explanation:	1 2 3 4 5 Explanation:

Assessment Sheet

Like a rolling stone

Critical Challenge

Critical Question

Should Jack, Ralph or Roger be charged with a homicide offense under the Criminal Code for the death of Piggy in *Lord of the Flies*?

Overview

The novel *Lord of the Flies* by William Golding offers a scathing look at human nature and society. In the novel a physically unappealing character named Piggy is killed by a group of boys who have become uncivilized. After reviewing the legal terms of manslaughter, first degree murder and second degree murder, students decide whether or not to charge Jack, Ralph or Roger with a homicide offense.

Requisite Tools

Background knowledge	• familiarity with the *Lord of the Flies* • familiarity of the terms first degree murder, second degree murder and manslaughter
Criteria for judgment	• the conditions for guilt for each of the homicide offenses
Critical thinking vocabulary	
Thinking strategies	• data chart
Habits of mind	

Suggested Activities

◆ Ask students if they have heard of the terms 'murder' and 'manslaughter.' In small groups, assign students to discuss the meaning of these types of homicide offenses, and to record their explanations of each. Invite a member from each group to read out their explanations of these terms. As a class, look at the *Criminal Code* definitions for murder.

familiarity with the types of homicide

- *Murder*: The unlawful killing of a person with malice—i.e., the active deliberate intention of doing an lawful action.

- *Manslaughter*: The unlawful killing of a person without malice.

Distinguish between *murder in the first degree*—deliberate killing with certain accompanying conditions (i.e., the victim was a police officer, the murder took place during a kidnapping) and *murder in the second degree*—deliberate killing where the accompanying conditions are not present.

◆ Distribute *Briefing Sheet: Conditions for Homicide* (Blackline Master) and talk students through the requirements for first degree murder, second degree murder and manslaughter.

the conditions for types of homicide

◆ Assign students to work individually to find evidence from the novel that could be used to charge Jack or Ralph or Roger with a homicide offense. Alternatively, organize students into groups where each member is assigned chapters to read, looking for evidence.

familiarity with the novel

◆ Suggest that students use *Data Chart: Evidence for Homicide* (Blackline Master) to record the information found about each character.

data chart

◆ Present the critical question:

> Should Jack, Ralph or Roger be charged with a homicide offense under the Criminal Code for the death of Piggy in *Lord of the Flies*?

Assign students to write a two-page essay where they are to argue whether there is enough evidence to charge any of the boys with a homicide offense. Suggest that students focus on two questions for each character:

- Is there sufficient evidence, based on the information in the data chart, to warrant a charge of first or second degree murder or manslaughter? If so, provide the evidence for the relevant charge.

- If there is not sufficient evidence, what conditions are missing?

Evaluation

◆ Assess the data chart on the amount of relevant evidence students found in the text for each of the conditions involved in determining whether a homicide was committed.

◆ Assess the essay on the following basis:
- plausibility of the evidence presented in light of the conditions required for the charge (or lack of charge);
- level of detail and clarity in presenting the evidence;
- proper format, spelling and punctuation.

Extension

◆ Invite students to take on the role of either defense counsel or Crown counsel and develop a case that they would present at the trial of either Jack, Ralph or Roger.

◆ Conduct a mock trial based on the evidence collected in this activity. Discuss with students the burden of proof required to establish guilt in criminal cases, namely that the person must be guilty beyond a reasonable doubt (i.e., any doubts about innocence must be based on reasons and not simply be imagined doubts).

Reference

Golding, William. (1954) *Lord of the Flies*. London: Faber & Faber Limited. (ISBN 0-19-8319703).

Conditions for homicide

The following definitions are loosely condensed from a variety of sources including the *Criminal Code of Canada*. These conditions do not identify all of the formal legal requirements for these offenses.

First Degree Murder

- when the act is planned and deliberate;
- when there is an arrangement under which money or anything of value passes or is intended to pass to another who assists or counsels another person to commit murder;
- when the victim is a law enforcement officer, acting in the course of his/her duties;
- when the death is caused by a person who committed or attempts to commit a hijacking or kidnapping, or commits or attempts to commit rape;
- when the person causing the murder has previously been convicted of either first or second degree murder.

Second Degree Murder

Any murder that is not first degree murder.

Manslaughter

Murder can be reduced to manslaughter if:

- the person who committed it did so in the heat of passion caused by sudden provocation (i.e., something or someone who provokes or "eggs" someone on);
- the person who committed it did so after receiving an act or insult that was sufficient to deprive an ordinary person of the power of self-control;
- the accused was heavily intoxicated;
- the accused did not have the mental capacity to form the specific intention (or conscious purpose) to commit murder;
- an unforeseen death arises through an assault and the accused did not anticipate the ensuing death.

Briefing Sheet

Evidence for homicide

Conditions for homicide	Jack	Ralph	Roger
First degree murder			
• planned and deliberate			
• money or valuables given			
• victim is law enforcement officer			
• involves hijacking, kidnapping or rape			
• was previously convicted of murder			
Reduced to manslaughter			
• heat of passion			
• over-powering insult			
• heavily intoxicated			
• mentally incapacity			
• unforeseen death			

Data Chart

Leader of the pack

Critical Challenge

Critical Question

Which character in *Lord of the Flies* has stronger leadership qualities: Jack or Ralph?

Overview

This is the first of two challenges which use William Golding's novel *Lord of the Flies* to deal with leadership. Students explore the attributes of good leaders and then match these against the qualities of two main characters in the novel, Ralph and Jack. Students discuss and eventually decide which of the two characters has the stronger leadership qualities.

Requisite Tools

Background knowledge	• familiarity with *Lord of the Flies*
Criteria for judgment	• attributes of good leadership
Critical thinking vocabulary	
Thinking strategies	• data chart
Habits of mind	

Suggested Activities

◆ To help students begin thinking about leadership qualities, ask members of the class to name several individuals they judge to be good leaders. Record these names down a column on the board.

data chart

◆ Organize students into small groups to consider the attributes possessed by these and other leaders. Distribute *Data Chart #1: Leadership Profiles* (Blackline Master) and invite students to identify two leaders at each of three levels of operation: the school, community and national/international level. For each leader, students should discuss and record one or two attributes that make this person stand out as a leader.

◆ Once completed, ask students to share information from their charts in a class discussion. While the discussion is progressing, list the attributes of good leadership down a second column on the board. On the basis of the class discussion, invite students to identify the five most important leadership attributes.

attributes of good leadership

◆ Distribute *Data Chart #2: Jack's and Ralph's Leadership* (Blackline Master) and ask students to copy this list of the five most important leadership attributes into the left-hand column on the Data Chart.

data chart

◆ Direct students individually to consult the novel looking for evidence that suggests whether or not Jack and Ralph possess these attributes. Students should record this evidence in the appropriate columns on *Data Chart #2*. Invite students to share their findings with other members of their group. On the basis of this evidence, each group is to rate on a scale of 1 to 3 the degree to which Jack and Ralph exhibit each of the agreed-upon attributes.

familiarity with the novel

◆ Once each group has completed *Data Chart #2*, present the critical question:

> Which character in *Lord of the Flies* has stronger leadership qualities, Jack or Ralph?

Organize students into a U-shaped classroom discussion to determine which of the two main characters possesses the better leadership qualities. Ask students to seat themselves in a "U" according to the position they take about the better leader: those who think Jack is the better leader sit at the top end of the U on one side of the room, those who are undecided are to take seats in the middle of the U, and those who think Ralph is the better leader are to sit on the other end of the U.

During the discussion encourage students to clarify their position and to offer reasons from the novel to support their views. Provide several opportunities for students to move their seats to match any changes in their position on the matter under discussion.

◆ As a culminating activity assign students to choose between Jack or Ralph as the character with the stronger leadership qualities and write a journal entry justifying this position.

Evaluation

◆ Assess the journal based on the following criteria:
- states a clear position;
- supports opinions in light of the agreed-upon attributes of a good leader;
- provides ample and accurate evidence from the novel;
- uses correct grammar, spelling and punctuation.

Extension

◆ Distinguish between a good and an effective leader. Consider whether Jack or Ralph is more effective as a leader.

◆ Evaluate Piggy's leadership qualities using the same process, and determine if Piggy could have emerged as a leader?

Reference

Golding, William. (1954). *Lord of the Flies*. London: Faber & Faber Limited. (ISBN 0-19-8319703).

Leadership profiles

Names of school leaders	Leadership qualities

Names of community leaders	Leadership qualities

Names of national/ international leaders	Leadership qualities
Martin Luther King Jr.	*He stood up for his beliefs* *even when they were unpopular.*

Data Chart #1

Jack's and Ralph's leadership

List the five most important attributes of good leadership in the column on the left. Look for evidence from the novel that suggests whether or not Jack and Ralph possess these attributes. Rate the extent to which each character exhibits these attributes on the following scale:

1 = Not at all   2 = Somewhat   3 = Definitely

Data Chart #2

Leadership qualities	JACK Evidence from the novel	rating	RALPH Evidence from the novel	rating
Respect for the ideas and opinions of others	Jack speaks out of turn, disregarding the conch	3 2 ①(1)	Ralph gives everyone the opportunity to hold the conch and speak	②③(3) 2 1
		3 2 1		3 2 1
		3 2 1		3 2 1
		3 2 1		3 2 1
		3 2 1		3 2 1
		3 2 1		3 2 1

Who said words can't kill you?

Critical Challenge

Critical Question

Which character in *Lord of the Flies* is the more powerful leader: Jack or Ralph?

Overview

This is the second part of two challenges about leadership using William Golding's novel *Lord of the Flies*. The characters who possess the best leadership qualities are not always the strongest leaders. This is also true with leaders in ordinary society. Often leaders find ways to become powerful to make up for their leadership deficiencies. In this lesson students examine the acquisition of power by using propaganda techniques. They examine the primary leaders in the novel, Ralph and Jack, and study how they use propaganda techniques to enhance their natural leadership skills. Students conclude their analysis of propaganda devices by writing about the most powerful leader in the novel.

Requisite Tools

Background knowledge	• familiarity with *Lord of the Flies*
Criteria for judgment	• effective use of propaganda devices
Critical thinking vocabulary	• persuasion • propaganda
Thinking strategies	• data chart
Habits of mind	

Suggested Activities

◆ Lead a class discussion about ways people gain power in everyday life. Discussion prompts might include strategies to manipulate people—such as:

- parents in order to break a family rule such as curfew;
- teachers in order to delay an exam;
- supervisors to get off work early.

◆ At the close of this discussion, ask students to analyze and then categorize these strategies for manipulating people in power. Define persuasion and propaganda and ask students to provide examples of each. Reconsider these strategies along a spectrum that begins with persuasion and ends with propaganda. Ask students to discuss the fine line where persuasion becomes propaganda.

persuasion & propaganda

◆ Ask students to identify techniques or devices used by propagandists and compile a list on the overhead projector or chalk board.

◆ When the student-generated list includes most of the devices defined in *Backgrounder: Propaganda Devices* (Blackline Master), distribute the sheet to students and ask them to highlight the propaganda devices presented in the discussion about manipulating parents, teachers or supervisors. Ask students to look at the remaining propaganda devices and identify situations in which these devices might be used.

effective propaganda devices

◆ Organize students to work in small groups to identify propaganda techniques used by characters in *Lord of the Flies* and record this information on *Data Chart: Propaganda in Lord of the Flies* (Blackline Master).

familiarity with the novel

◆ When groups have completed their charts, ask group representatives to use data collected to answer the following questions in a class discussion:

- Which character stands out as the greater propagandist?
- To what degree are the propaganda devices used successfully?
- What techniques are used most frequently in the novel? Why are they effective?
- How do these techniques enhance the individual leadership styles?

◆ Present the critical question:

Which character in *Lord of the Flies* was the more powerful leader: Jack or Ralph?

◆ Prior to the writing assignment, ask students to generate criteria for assessing a response journal or short essay on leadership qualities.

Ask students to answer this question in a response journal.

Evaluation

◆ Evaluate the writing based on the following criteria:
  • evidence of understanding of propaganda devices;
  • logical and effective organization of ideas;
  • use of quotes, examples or references to support points;
  • mechanical correctness.

Extension

◆ Assign students to design a campaign poster for one of the leaders in *Lord of the Flies* (Ralph or Jack) that demonstrates their ability to use propaganda techniques. Ask students to consider both a slogan and a visual display. Evaluate these posters on visual effectiveness and the successful use of propaganda techniques.

◆ Hold an election in the class with Jack and Ralph running as opposing candidates. Ask students to write election speeches, write campaign pamphlets and design television advertisements. Evaluate students on the effective use of propaganda devices to persuade the electorate.

◆ Adapt this lesson to other novels that focus on characters who manipulate others using propaganda devices (e.g., *Animal Farm* and *1984* by George Orwell).

◆ If students have now completed both critical challenges on *Lord of the Flies*, ask students to combine the idea of leadership qualities and powerful leadership into a longer writing assignment based on the critical question: Which character in *Lord of the Flies* is the better overall leader: Jack or Ralph?

Reference

Golding, William. (1954). *Lord of the Flies*. London: Faber & Faber Limited. (ISBN 0-19-8319703).

Propaganda devices

Selection   Out of a mass of complex facts, propagandists select only those facts that suit their purposes.

Repetition   If a statement is repeated often enough, it will eventually be remembered by the audience (e.g., It's a free country).

Lies and half-truths   Falsehood is a major propaganda tool. A former American senator said, "Truth is the first casualty of war." Truth is also the first casualty in propaganda because the propagandist's purpose is to win audience support and is sometimes willing to lie to get it.

Rhetorical questions   These are questions which do not require an answer from the reader or listener because the answer is obvious. Often a rhetorical question is answered by the speaker in the next sentence (e.g., Do you want to be a failure all your life?).

Targetting the enemy   Presenting information which identifies an enemy, real or imagined, in order to win support is a common propaganda device. This tactic is used to unify a group and direct its aggression outwards by scapegoating (e.g., Hitler blamed Jews for the collapse of the German economy in the 1930s).

Assertion   Propagandists rarely argue, instead they make bold statements to defend their position. During the cold war in the 1950s, anti-Communist politicians promoted their position in slogans (e.g., "Better dead than Red").

Bandwagon   Propagandists encourage their audience to do or think something by saying that everyone else believes, does or owns something. This tactic feeds on and satisfies the human need to belong to a group and fit in.

Comparisons   Propagandists compare themselves (for better or worse) to others in order to amplify their favourable values, qualities, skills or actions.

Embarassment   Propagandists sometimes present embarassing stories or information about the opponents or enemy in order to make them look foolish or undesirable. Sometimes the information is exaggerated or distorted so as to unite the target audience against the opponents or enemy.

Humour   Propogandists use humour to become friendly with audience members and get on the side of the audience in order to show them that the propagandist is just like them, a regular person. The objective is to win the audience's trust for later manipulation.

Backgrounder

Propaganda in Lord of the Flies

Propaganda device	First example		Second example	
1. Selection		J R		J R
2. Repetition		J R		J R
3. Lying		J R		J R
4. Rhetorical question		J R		J R
5. Target the enemy		J R		J R
6. Assertion		J R		J R
7. Bandwagon		J R		J R
8. Comparisons		J R		J R
9. Embarassment		J R		J R
10. Humour	*Jack makes fun of Piggy by calling him "fatty"*	(J) R	*Ralph tells the boys to call Piggy "Piggy"*	J (R)

Data Chart

A question of pride?

Critical Challenge

Critical Question

Was Al a fool for turning down the job?

Overview

The protagonist Al Condraj must make a moral decision in the short story *The Parsley Garden* by William Saroyan. The plot involves a young man from a low income, single parent family who shoplifts a hammer. He feels ashamed and humiliated by his action and, after working off his debt, he is faced with the decision to continue working and swallow his pride, or to continue on with his meager way of living, with his value system intact. Students make a judgment about Al's decision not to take a job. They then learn to think about counter-arguments as they re-evaluate their initial assessment of Al's decision.

Requisite Tools

Background knowledge	• familiarity with the short story "The Parsley Garden"
Criteria for judgment	• supporting position with textual evidence
Critical thinking vocabulary	• counter-argument
Thinking strategies	• data chart
Habits of mind	

Suggested Activities

◆ Before reading *The Parsley Garden* by William Saroyan, divide the class into four groups. Without any comment (so as not to lead students), give each group one of the following statements and have them act out a "scene" that relates to the story.

- You go to your mother for advice and she tells you to "shut up."
- You get caught shoplifting.
- Your boss is rude to you.
- You own a store and you are constantly being ripped off. You catch someone stealing from you.

◆ After each "performance" open a discussion about the choices that were made during the presentation (e.g., you are irate with the "thief" who stole from you therefore, you yell and scream at him). Ask students to imagine that there is a plausible, perfectly innocent explanation for the incident. What might this explanation be: Why might it be understandable for a mother tell a child to "shut up?" Why might it be justified that someone would shoplift? These scenes and the follow-up discussion should elicit the thoughts and emotions that the characters in the short story may have felt and create an appropriate mind-set for the challenge.

◆ Ask students to read the short story *The Parsley Garden*.

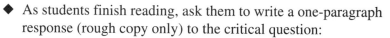

familiarity with the story

◆ As students finish reading, ask them to write a one-paragraph response (rough copy only) to the critical question:

   Was Al a fool for turning down the job?

◆ Before asking students to share their reasons for their answer to the critical question, designate two small groups as blackboard recorders—one group recording the NO side arguments; the other group recording the YES side arguments.

◆ After students have generated various arguments for both sides, introduce the concept of 'counter-argument'—that there may be opposing reasons which could explain or counter the justification offered. Illustrate this concept by offering possible counter-arguments to a few of the reasons students offered. Encourage students to offer additional counter-arguments and arguments which counter your counter-arguments.

counter-argument

◆ Distribute *Data Chart #1 No: Al Is Not a Fool* (Blackline Master) to those students who supported this view in their one paragraph response, and distribute *Data Chart #2: Yes: Al Is a Fool* (Blackline Master) to those holding this other view. Assign students to small groups ensuring wherever possible that there is at least one representative from each side in each group. Each student is to complete his or her own Data Chart during or immediately after conferring with others in their group.

data chart

◆ Provide an opportunity for students from both sides to share with other groups their counter-arguments and counter counter-arguments.

◆ Invite students to revisit their initial one-paragraph response to the critical question:

Was Al a fool for turning down the job?

Students are to write a more extensive one-page response, where the focus is on exploring counter-arguments and counter counter-arguments to their position. While revising, encourage students to explain how or why they made any changes in their initial opinion. Students should submit their original paragraph with their revised one-page response.

Evaluation

◆ Assess the one-page response on the following criteria:
- use of relevant examples from the text to support position;
- offer plausible counter-arguments to reasons for their position;
- counter the counter-arguments with plausible arguments;
- clearly written;
- writing is free of mechanical errors.

Extension

◆ If students have worked with poetry, invite them to write a narrative poem (ballad) recounting the events in the short story. Students can write this from any character's point of view (e.g., Al Condraj, store owners, Al's mother).

◆ Suggest that students identify an important moral or personal decision they will face in the upcoming months or years and think of reasons for and against and possible counter-arguments to all of the reasons they identify.

Reference

Saroyan, William. (1987). "The Parsley Garden". In *Inside Stories I*. (Glen Kirkland & Richard Davies, Eds.) Toronto: Harcourt Brace. (ISBN 0-7747-1271-6).

No! Al is not a fool

Possible reasons why Al is NOT a fool	Counter-arguments	Countering the counter-arguments
He's keeping his pride intact by not taking the job.	His family could use the money.	Money isn't the most important thing in life.

Data Chart #1

Yes! Al is a fool

Possible reasons why Al IS a fool	Counter-arguments	Countering the counter-arguments

Data Chart #2

Who done it?

Critical Challenge

Critical Task

Write an epilogue to *The Moose and the Sparrow* explaining the circumstances surrounding Moose Maddon's death.

Overview

In *The Moose and the Sparrow*, by Hugh Garner, the character Cecil is a slight young man who works at a logging camp during his summer breaks from University. Despite his pleasing personality and strong work ethic, Cecil is constantly being tormented by Moose Maddon—a man who is seemingly threatened by Cecil's intelligence. Moose has an unfortunate accident and the question is whether or not Moose's death was accidental. (There is speculation that perhaps Cecil is responsible.) Students must decide on the basis of evidence from the text whether or not the death was accidental. They then write an epilogue using evidence from the text to present their account of the death of Moose Maddon.

Requisite Tools

Background knowledge	• familiarity with the story *The Moose and the Sparrow*	
Criteria for judgment	• plausibility of evidence from the text to support explanation • weight of evidence	
Critical thinking vocabulary		bias
Thinking strategies	• data chart	
Habits of mind	• attention to detail	

Suggested Activities

◆ Invite students to read the short story "The Moose and the Sparrow". Discuss as a class how Moose might have died: accidentally or at Cecil's hands.

familiarity with the story

◆ Invite students to take on the role of detective and, like all good detectives, they must pay close attention to detail. Emphasize the need to consider any shred of evidence and all sources of evidence, including that from all characters.

attention to detail

◆ Each student is to compile an ongoing list of evidence for both the accident and the murder hypothesis. See *Data Chart: Evidence Chart* (Blackline Master) for an example.

data chart

◆ Suggest that students begin their investigation by completing in small groups *Student Activity: Character Profile* (Blackline Master) to explore the traits of both Cecil and Moose for clues as to the most plausible explanation for Moose's death.

◆ Invite students to consider, in their small groups, any clues that the narrator of the story (Pop Anderson) gives which suggest that Moose's death might be accidental and, alternatively, that it might be murder.

◆ Encourage students to look for additional evidence. Once students have collected and recorded their evidence, ask them to consider which hypothesis is the most plausible, that is, which option is most supported by the evidence they have found?

weight of plausible evidence

◆ Once students have formed their opinion, arrange the class into a 'U' formation with students who believe the death was accidental on one end, those who believe it was murder on the other, and those who are uncertain in the bottom of the 'U'. Students share ideas in an informal debate situation. (Some guideline for control may be necessary, such as only the students holding the chalk brush may speak.) Periodically encourage students to change their position along the 'U'. By the end of the discussion each student should have formed an opinion about the most plausible cause of Moose's death.

Discuss the meaning and purpose of an epilogue. Students must include evidence from the text to support their view and must write in the same style as the story.

◆ Present the critical task:

Write an epilogue to *The Moose and the Sparrow* explaining the circumstances surrounding Moose Maddon's death.

Evaluation

◆ Assess each student's Data Chart for the extent of plausible evidence and the degree of insight/imagination in identifying shreds of evidence.

◆ Assess each student's epilogue on the following bases:

• extent and plausibility of evidence from text to support the identified cause of Moose's death;

• degree to which the epilogue is written in the style of the original story;

• proper format, spelling and punctuation.

Extension

◆ Present evidence in a mock trial.

◆ Present a mock trial where the jury has not read the story; they only listen to the cases. Members of the jury must support why they voted as they did. They should go back and now read the story and formulate their opinions. Do they agree with their verdict, or would they change it?

◆ Use several pieces of short story writing but with differing styles and ask students to develop their own.

Reference

Garner, Hugh. (1980). "The Moose and the Sparrow." In *Singing Under Ice* (M. Grace Mersereau, Ed.). Toronto: Gage. (ISBN 0-7715-1678-9).

Evidence chart

PG. #	WAS ACCIDENTAL	WAS MURDER

Data Chart

Character profile

Character: **Cecil**

1. What do we know about Cecil's character that could make us suspicious of him? Consider the following:

    a) personality

    b) actions

    c) physical possessions

    d) how others act toward Cecil

Character: **Moose**

1. What do we know about Moose's character that would lead us to believe the death was his own fault? Consider the following:

    a) personality

    b) actions

    c) physical possessions

    d) how others act toward Moose

Daytime friends are night time lovers

Critical Challenge

Critical Task

Write Ann's diary entry after her husband's death from two different positions: one which points to her unfaithfulness, and one to her faithfulness.

Overview

The short story *The Painted Door* by Sinclair Ross is about a husband and wife who are facing difficulty in their marriage. Ann, the wife in the story, feels an attraction to her husband's friend Steven. As the story progresses Sinclair Ross is deliberately ambiguous about Ann's fidelity. Students first discuss what it means to be unfaithful and then examine Ann's fidelity or lack thereof. The culminating activity is to write two diary entries from Ann's point of view: one which points to her infidelity and the other which points to her fidelity. By doing this students also learn about counter-argument.

Requisite Tools

Background knowledge	• familiarity with the story *The Painted Door*
Criteria for judgment	• features of being "unfaithful" (e.g., intentionally hurt others, act behind the back of others)
Critical thinking vocabulary	• counter-argument • point of view
Thinking strategies	• data chart
Habits of mind	

Suggested Activities

◆ As a homework assignment, assign students to read *The Painted Door* by Sinclair Ross.

familiarity with the story

◆ Ask students to think of a time when a friend was unfaithful to them. Frame unfaithfulness broadly to include examples such as a friend telling a secret to a third party, boyfriend/girlfriend break up, a friend not keeping a commitment, etc.

features of being unfaithful

◆ In a class discussion or in small groups ask students to brainstorm key features of "unfaithfulness." Suggest some of the following features:
  • an action with the intention to hurt another person;
  • an action done behind someone's back;
  • an attack on a belief or event that a person values highly;
  • a violation of a mutual understanding between the two individuals.

◆ Ask students to summarize the previous two activities that explore the definition of "unfaithfulness" by writing a personal definition of the word and a list of criteria to test unfaithfulness. Explain that at a later point in time, they may decide to add qualifications to this definition or modify it.

◆ Introduce the notion of point of view.

point of view

◆ Organize a "human graph" to engage students in further exploration of the fine line between faithfulness and unfaithfulness. On a long wall in the classroom post the numbers 1 through 5, creating five zones. Present each of the following questions and ask students to take a "stand" that corresponds to their belief. Assign Number 1 to the position of strongest agreement and Number 5 to strongest disagreement. Once students have lined up in front of the number most closely representing their positions, a human graph will be evident to the class. Follow each question with an opportunity for students to justify their position on the human graph and a chance to reposition themselves after hearing others speak. After each question ask students to discuss how their present position fits their criteria for unfaithfulness.

Would you consider your spouse or partner to be unfaithful if
. . .

- he/she shared intimate thoughts with a person outside the relationship?
- he/she admitted an attraction to a person of the opposite sex?
- he/she admitted fantasizing about someone of the opposite sex?
- he/she had sex with another partner?

◆ Ask students to review their personal definition and list of criteria for unfaithfulness. Explain that this lesson will use the class-generated criteria for the term "unfaithful" to judge Ann's unfaithfulness. Ask students to copy down the class-established criteria for unfaithfulness.

◆ Discuss the ambiguity of the Sinclair Ross' story and introduce the concept of inference. Using *Data Chart: Ann's Unfaithfulness* (Blackline Master) and the criteria given by the class, determine if Ann was unfaithful to John. Ask students to provide quotes from the text that support their opinions.

data chart

◆ After sharing some of their findings, introduce and define counter-argument. Ask students to find one quote to support the 'other side' and record this on *Data Chart: Ann's Unfaithfulness* (Blackline Master).

counter-argument

◆ Use a T-Chart (on the chalkboard or overhead); label the first column *Ann is Faithful* and a second column *Ann is Unfaithful*. Complete the T-Chart with the quotes students have found.

data chart

◆ Once the quotes are on the chalkboard or on an overhead transparency, ask students to take one of the two positions: Ann is faithful or Ann is unfaithful. It may be necessary to allow a position for those students who are undecided. Arrange class-room seating so that people who have chosen each of these positions are seated in one group or the other.

◆ Discuss the quotes on the board and ask students to defend their position. Present the counter-positions by using the criteria in the chart (for example, Did Ann know her action would hurt her husband?). Allow students to move positions throughout the discussion. Point out that some quotes may appear to support both sides of the T-Chart, and discuss Ross's use of ambiguity.

◆ After students have had an opportunity to discuss their positions, direct them to return to their usual classroom seats and present the critical task:

Write Ann's diary entry after her husband's death from two different positions: one which points to her unfaithfulness, and one to her faithfulness.

Encourage students to support each position with examples from the text.

Evaluation

◆ Assess the Data Chart based on students' ability to
  • identify relevant actions and thoughts;
  • explain how the action and thoughts suggest faithfulness/unfaithfulness to her husband.

◆ Assess the diary entries based on students' ability to
  • use incidents in the text to argue that the criteria of faithfulness/unfaithfulness have been met;
  • make counter-arguments from a set of facts;
  • convincingly argue both the faithful and unfaithful positions.

Extension

◆ Assign students to reflect on the following questions either in discussion or writing:

  • What are some benefits of writing ambiguously?

  • When is ambiguity acceptable? Desirable?

  • What type of story development requires ambiguity?

◆ Write a story that has a purposely ambiguous development.

◆ Watch the film version of *The Painted Door* and examine the director's portrayal of Ann. Ask students to determine if the film director portrayed her as faithful or unfaithful? Use *Data Chart: Ann's Unfaithfulness* (Blackline Master) to analyze the film.

References

The text version of *The Painted Door* by Sinclair Ross can be found in many anthologies. Two easily available sources are:

Kirkland, Glen and Davies, Richard. (1993). *Inside Stories For Senior Students*. Toronto: Harcourt Brace. (ISBN 0-7747-1408-5).

MacNeill and Sorestad. (1973). *Tigers of the Snow*. Scarborough, ON: Nelson Canada. (ISBN 0-17-633043-7).

A video adaptation of *The Painted Door* has been made by the Provincial Educational Media Center. It is part of their Canadian Literature Series.

Ann's unfaithfulness

Instructions: For each of the criteria established for unfaithfulness explain whether or not Ann was being unfaithful to John.

ANN'S ACTIONS & THOUGHTS	Are intended to hurt person	Carried out behind the person's back	Attack the person's beliefs	Violate mutual understanding
Dances with Steven at the barn dance				
Allows Steven to visit in John's absence				
"her eyes were fanatic, believing desperately, fixed upon him as if to exclude all else, as if to find justification"				

CRITERIA FOR UNFAITHFULNESS

Data Chart

Baseball is life . . . the rest is just details

Critical Challenge

Critical Question

Is the metaphor of "baseball is life" in the poem *The Base Stealer* a powerful one?

Overview

The poem, *The Base Stealer,* by Robert Francis catches a crucial type of play in baseball. It can be seen to suggest many other things–life, decision making and growing up. Students read the poem with the title removed, hypothesize what it is about, and then explore the poem as an extended metaphor.

Requisite Tools

Background knowledge	• familarity with the poem *The Base Stealer*
	• understanding metaphor
Criteria for judgment	• criteria for a powerful metaphor (e.g., is apt, offers insight, is original)
Critical thinking vocabulary	
Thinking strategies	• data chart
Habits of mind	

Suggested Activities

◆ Organize students into small groups. On an overhead, show the poem, *The Base Stealer*, by Robert Francis with the title removed and ask each group to brainstorm the title of this poem. This poem is found on *"Transparency #1: Untitled"* (Blackline Master).

familiarity with poem

◆ Distribute chart paper, and ask each group to write a title that reflects the content, theme or mood of the poem. Invite students to record on the chart paper quotes from the poem to support their idea. Suggest that students re-think their title if appropriate.

◆ Post each group's chart paper on the classroom wall, and discuss the student evidence. Provide students with the original title and discuss how it fits the poem.

◆ Review the meaning of "metaphor." Discuss whether or not *The Base Stealer* is explicitly about a baseball player. Ask students to look beyond the literal meaning and suggest metaphorical interpretations of the poem.

understanding metaphor

◆ Ask students to complete the first three columns of *Data Chart: Metaphorical Analysis of "The Base Stealer"* (Blackline Master) to demonstrate an understanding of how the poem works on two levels of meaning. Students should look for quotes from the poem and indicate parallels between baseball and life.

data chart

◆ Explore with students the criteria of a powerful metaphor. Possible suggestions include

• is apt (Does it apply to the new context?);

• offers insight (Does it reveal thoughtful or subtle ideas about the topic?);

• is original (Is it a novel or fresh comparsion?).

criteria for powerful metaphors

◆ Test *The Base Stealer* against the criteria for powerful metaphors. Assign students to complete the remaining columns—Criteria for Powerful Metaphors—of *Data Chart: Metaphorical Analysis of "The Base Stealer"* (Blackline Master) and discuss student interpretations.

◆ Present the critical question:

Is the metaphor of "baseball is life" in the poem *The Base Stealer* a powerful one?

Invite students to respond by indicating the degree—along a continuum from "extremely powerful" to "very weak"—to which "baseball is life" is a powerful metaphor.

Evaluation

◆ Assess the completed Data Charts on students' ability to:

• identify appropriate quotes;

• interpret the literal meaning and figurative meaning from the poem;

• provide plausible reasons to support their assessments or how well the parallels between baseball and life meet the criteria of a powerful metaphor.

Extension

◆ Ask students to write an extended life metaphor, demonstrating the ability to write a passage on two different levels of meaning. Expect students to keep the criteria for powerful metaphors in mind. Evaluate these metaphors using the criteria. Suggest that the metaphor have an interesting title, offering examples such as.

Life is a candle . . .

Life is a salad bar . . .

Life is a rodeo . . .

Life is a roller coaster . . .

Life is a pair of shoes . . .

◆ Arrange for peer evaluation of student-created metaphors, using the criteria for powerful metaphors.

◆ Assign students to write a life metaphor involving another sport using the poem "The Base Stealer" as a model.

◆ Study the poem "Ball Game" by Richard Eberhart and compare it to "The Base Stealer." This poem is found on *Transparency #2: Ball Game* (Blackline Master).

References

Francis, Robert. (1991). "The Base Stealer." In *Departures: Reflections in Poetry* (Edited by James Barry). Scarborough, ON: Nelson. (ISBN 0-17-603717-9)

Eberhart, Richard. (1992). "Ball Game." In *Sports in Literature* (Edited by Brice Emra). Chicago: National Textbook Company.

Untitled

Poised between going on and back, pulled
Both ways taut like a tightrope-walker,
Fingertips pointing the opposites.
Now bouncing tiptoe like a dropped ball
Or a kid skipping rope, come on, come on,
Running a scattering of steps sidewise,
How he teeters, skitters, tingles, teases,
Taunts them, hovers like an ecstatic bird,
He's only flirting, crowd him, crowd him,
Delicate, delicate, delicate, delicate—now!

—Robert Francis

The Ball Game

Caught off first, he leaped to run to second, but

Then struggled back to first.

He left first because of a natural desire

To leap, to get on with the game.

When you jerk to run to second

You do not necessarily think of a home run.

You want to go on. You want to get to the next stage,

The entire soul is bent on second base.

The fact is that the mind flashes

Faster in action than the muscles can move.

Dramatic! Off first, taut, heading for second,

In a split second, total realization,

Heading for first. Head first! Legs follow fast.

You struggle back to first with victor effort

As, even, after a life of effort and chill,

One flashes back to the safety of childhood,

To that strange place where one had first begun.

—*Richard Eberhart*

Metaphorical analysis of "The Base Stealer"

Data Chart

QUOTE	PARALLELS		CRITERIA FOR POWERFUL METAPHORS		
	Relates to baseball because	Relates to life because	Aptness or Applicability?	Insightfulness or Subtlety?	Originality?
Poised between going on and back	It talks about stealing a base	Life is full of difficult decisions that pull us in opposing directions			
Pulled both ways like a tightrope-walker					
Now bouncing tiptoe like a dropped ball					

Back to the future

Critical Challenge

Critical Question

Which Shakespearean theme is most relevant to our modern society?

Overview

Many students question the relevance of studying Shakespeare. This challenge links themes found in Shakespearean plays to issues in modern society. Students evaluate the degree to which themes in *A Midsummer Night's Dream* are applicable to their own lives.

Requisite Tools

Background knowledge	• familiarity with the play • definition of 'theme'	
Criteria for judgment	• criteria for establishing greatest relevance to their lives (e.g., widest applicability, most pertinent)	
Critical thinking vocabulary		
Thinking strategies		
Habits of mind		

Suggested Activities

◆ In class discussion review the definition of "theme" and ask students to brainstorm themes found in Shakespeare's *A Midsummer Night's Dream*. Suggest such themes as parenting, love, power in relationships and the supernatural/magic if they are not raised in discussion.

definition of theme

◆ Assign students to complete *Data Chart #1: Theme Comparison Chart* (Blackline Master) beginning with the themes generated in class discussion. Instruct students to describe, in the first column, how the theme appears in the play and describe, in the second column, how the same issue appears in modern society.

◆ Once completed, discuss the charts with the class. Begin with questions such as:

- Which issues seem the easiest to link between the past and present?

- Which issues seem the most difficult to link between the past and present?

◆ Divide students into small groups. Provide each group with scissors, current newspapers and news magazines, glue, and a large piece of construction paper. Direct each group to search through the current newspapers and news magazines to find articles, headlines and/or pictures of current issues to compose a collage that illustrates the link between the present and Shakespearean themes.

◆ When the group activity is completed ask groups to share their posters and explain the clippings they selected.

◆ Assign students to complete *Data Chart #2: Comparing Shakespeare's Time with the Present* (Blackline Master). Use this as a foundation for a discussion to determine which notion is of greatest relevance. Ask students which of these themes has the most extensive and pertinent applicability in today's life and why. Invite students to offer other relevant features.

criteria for relevance

◆ Present the critical question:

Which Shakespearean theme is most relevant to our modern society?

Students should write a short essay to explain and defend their answer. Suggest that students explore why their theme is more extensive and pertinent to today's life than any of the other themes.

Evaluation

◆ Evaluate students' posters and/or individual comparison statement sheets based on the quantity and quality (e.g., insight, depth of comparison) of relevant links students make between the past and present.

◆ Evaluate responses to the critical challenge on how students use informaton from the data charts to explain why their choice meets the criteria for greatest relevance to modern society.

Extension

◆ Hold a debate with the resolution: "*A Midsummer Night's Dream* is still relevant to modern society."

◆ Translate a Shakespearean scene into modern English demonstrating that the play is relevant to modern society.

Theme comparison chart

	SHAKESPEARE'S TIME	CONTEMPORARY SOCIETY
Parenting		
Love		
Power		
Supernatural		

Data Chart #1

Comparing Shakespeare's time with the present

SIMILARITIES	DIFFERENCES
Parenting in Shakespeare's time is *similar* to today because	*Parenting* in Shakespeare's time is *different* from today because
Love in Shakespeare's time is *similar* to today because	*Love* in Shakespeare's time is *different* from today because
Power in Shakespeare's time is *similar* to today because	*Power* in Shakespeare's time is different is *different* from today because
The supernatural in Shakespeare's time is *similar* to today because	*The supernatural* in Shakespeare's time is *different* from today because

Data Chart #2

Dumb and dumber

Critical Challenge

Critical Question

To what extent are Romeo and Juliet victims of fate?

Overview

The play *Romeo and Juliet* by William Shakespeare is a romantic tragedy that focuses on the lives of two teens as they meet and fall in love. They are victims of a long standing family feud preventing a relationship between these two lovers This fate, combined with a series of events, leads to tragic deaths. Students examine the events leading to the deaths of Romeo and Juliet and to what degree these events were caused by fate (beyond their control) or by free will (the result of personal decisions).

Requisite Tools

Background knowledge	• familiarity with Shakespeare's *Romeo and Juliet*	
Criteria for judgment	• degree to which events are the result of fate or free will	
Critical thinking vocabulary		
Thinking strategies	• data chart	
Habits of mind		

Suggested Activities

◆ As a class invite students to identify some of the major events in their lives (students might suggest, for example, a team championship, special trip, major surgery, personal accomplishment).

◆ When the list is sufficiently developed, assign students to select one event from the list and complete the first two columns of *Data Chart #1: Major Event Lead-up* (Blackline Master). Direct students to analyze the major event in terms of a series of lesser events leading to the end result. As illustrated below, ask students to explain why or how each minor event is linked to the major event.

data chart

Minor event	Link to major event
Mr. Harvey was my grade 8 basketball coach	*His excellent coaching helped me learn proper skills at a young age and thus I was able to develop more fully which made it possible to play professionally.*

◆ Introduce and discuss the concepts of *fate* (circumstances beyond an individual's control) and *free will* (actions resulting directly from an individual's choices). Invite students to come up with simple, everyday examples of fate (e.g., The electricity fails overnight, your electric alarm does not go off and you miss a test?) and of free will (e.g., Because you chose to go to a movie instead of studying for a test, you are ill prepared and therefore fail the test.). Invite students to volunteer events they have listed on their Data Chart and to indicate to what extent these minor events are the instances of free will or of fate.

Criteria for fated and free actions

Encourage students to see that free will and fate are very much opposing ends of a continuum and that it is likely that elements of fate and free will co-exist in many events.

◆ Revisit *Data Chart #1: Major Event Lead-up* and ask students to complete the third column by indicating the degree to which the minor event is the result of free will or of fate. Conclude the activity by inviting students to present and discuss the elements of fate or free will in various minor events listed on their Data Chart.

◆ Organize students into pairs or groups of three to analyze the role of fate and free will in *Romeo and Juliet* by compiling *Data Chart #2: Fate or Free Will?* (Blackline Master). Instruct students to complete column one by describing an event from the specified scenes that eventually led to the death of Romeo or Juliet.

familiarity with the play

◆ On the second page of Data Chart #2 students are to identify events from a scene of their choice. Next, students are to complete column two by indicating how or why the event contributed to the deaths of Romeo or Juliet. In column three, students are to indicate the degree to which the event is the result of fate or free will.

◆ After students have completed Data Chart #2, present the critical question:

> To what extent are Romeo and Juliet victims of fate?

In their small groups students must decide their overall rating on how strongly fate influences the outcome of the play.

◆ Ask a representative from each group to share its conclusion with the class. Discuss any disagreements about whether events are the result of fate or free will, and invite students to justify their overall rating of the play's outcome.

Evaluation

◆ Assess Data Charts #1 and #2 on the following criteria:
- ability to identify relevant events that contribute to the final outcome;
- ability to explain the link between the event and the end result;
- ability to provide plausible justifications for their rating of the degree of fate or free will involved.

Extension

◆ Ask students to alter a few minor events in *Romeo and Juliet* and then write a summary version of the play in modern language illustrating how the alteration of an event could change the outcome of the story.

◆ Discuss the term "tragedy" as understood by students. Present the class with the definition found in a literary reference book (e.g., *Literary Terms: A Dictionary* - K. Beckson and A. Ganz, 1975). Discuss whether or not *Romeo and Juliet* should be classified as a tragedy.

Major event lead-up

Major Event: _____ (the final outcome)

List minor events	Explain how or why event is linked to final outcome	Indicate degree of fate/ free will involved
		Fate Free Will
		1 2 3 4 5
		1 2 3 4 5
		1 2 3 4 5
		1 2 3 4 5
		1 2 3 4 5
		1 2 3 4 5

Data Chart #1

Fate or free will?

Describe minor event from *Romeo and Juliet*	Explain how or why it contributed to the deaths of Romeo and Juliet	Indicate degree of fate/ free will involved
		Fate Free Will
Act 1, Sc. 5		1 2 3 4 5
Act 2, Sc. 2		1 2 3 4 5
Act 2, Sc. 3		1 2 3 4 5
Act 2, Sc. 6		1 2 3 4 5
Act 3, Sc. 1		1 2 3 4 5

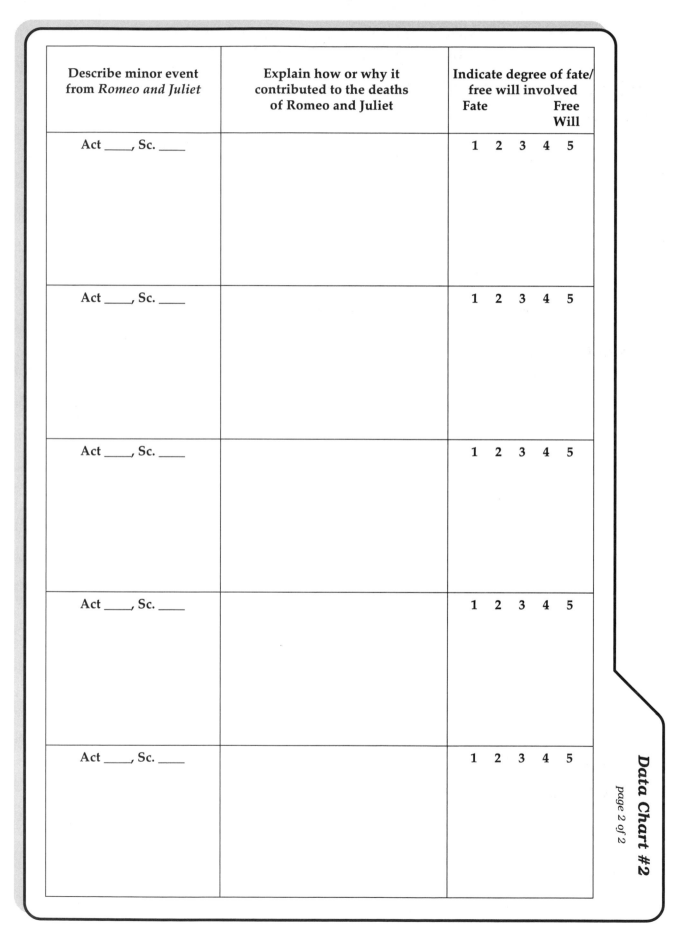

Describe minor event from *Romeo and Juliet*	Explain how or why it contributed to the deaths of Romeo and Juliet	Indicate degree of fate/ free will involved Fate Free Will
Act ____, Sc. ____		1 2 3 4 5
Act ____, Sc. ____		1 2 3 4 5
Act ____, Sc. ____		1 2 3 4 5
Act ____, Sc. ____		1 2 3 4 5
Act ____, Sc. ____		1 2 3 4 5

Data Chart #2
page 2 of 2

"Quote, unquote"

Critical Challenge

Critical Task

Select two significant quotations for inclusion in an end-of-unit literature test.

Overview

This critical challenge can be used at any grade level with any piece of literature. This lesson focusses on Shakespeare's play *Macbeth*. Students explore the criteria for powerful and significant literary quotations and then search the text looking for two quotes that satisfy these criteria. The class then judges the best among those quotes for inclusion in the culminating test for the unit.

Requisite Tools

Background knowledge	• familiarity with *Macbeth*
Criteria for judgment	• criteria for a significant quotation (e.g., advances the plot, reveals insight about a character, contains strong imagery)
Critical thinking vocabulary	
Thinking strategies	• data chart
Habits of mind	

Suggested Activities

◆ Brainstorm with the class criteria that should be considered when a teacher selects a quotation for analysis on a test and expects students to identify the speaker and the significance of the quote. Ask students what a quote should contain for it to be an appropriate question for analysis by students. Encourage the class to consider the following criteria:

criteria for significant quotation

- The quote advances the plot or is at a turning point.
- The quote reveals a main character.
- The quote contains strong imagery which adds to the atmosphere of the play.

◆ Assemble students into five groups. Prepare as an overhead *Transparency: Quotes from Macbeth* and distribute to each student a copy of *Student Activity #1: Evaluating a Quote* (Blackline Masters). Assign each group one of the quotes from the overhead and ask them to spend approximately 10 minutes evaluating their assigned quote in light of the criteria just discussed.

data chart

◆ After the groups have recorded the results of their evaluation on the chart *Student Activity #1*, invite them to present the quote to the whole class and justify their rating. Encourage students to comment on the ratings assigned by other groups if they disagree with the rating.

◆ Assign each group an Act from the play. They are to find two new significant quotes which they would recommend for inclusion on an end-of-unit test. Each group is to submit their recommended quotes with a page reference and a brief justification. Prepare a master list of recommended quotes.

familiarity with the play

◆ Duplicate and distribute a copy of the 10 recommended quotes to each student and present the critical task:

> Select two powerful and significant quotations for inclusion in an end-of-unit literature test.

◆ Using *Student Activity #2: Student Ballot* (Blackline Master) invite students individually to decide upon and justify their "vote" for the best two recommended quotes in light of the criteria set at the beginning of the class. Explain that student-voted quotes may be used on the actual unit test.

Evaluation

◆ Evaluate the "Students Ballots" on the following basis:
  • use of the criteria in justifying their selection;
  • quality of supporting reasons for their choices.

Quotes from Macbeth

1. (From Act 1)

    For brave Macbeth well he deserves the name
    Disdaining Fortune, with his brandished steel
    Which smoked with bloody execution,
    Like valour's minion carved out his passage
    Till he faced the slave.

2. (From Act 1)

    If chance will have me king why chance may crown me,
    without my stir.

3. (From Act 2)

    Will all great Neptune's ocean wash this blood
    clean from my hand? No, this my hand will rather
    the multitudinous seas incarnadine,
    making the green one red.

4. (From Act 2)

    Glamis hath murder'd sleep: and therefore Cawdor
    Shall sleep no more: Macbeth shall sleep no more!

5. (From Act 3)

    Ere we will eat our meal in fear, and sleep
    in the affliction of these terrible dreams
    that shake us nightly: better be with the dead.

Transparency

Evaluating a quote

Copy the quote assigned to your group on the first set of lines; then rate it in light of each of the criteria established in class. Explain your rating in the column on the right.

Quote: _____

_____

_____

Criterion Rating	Justification
advances plot Not at all Somewhat Definitely 1 2 3	
reveals character Not at all Somewhat Definitely 1 2 3	
imagery adds to atmosphere Not at all Somewhat Definitely 1 2 3	
other (specify) Not at all Somewhat Definitely 1 2 3	
other (specify) Not at all Somewhat Definitely 1 2 3	

Student Activity #1

Student ballot

Instructions: Vote for two quotes from the list of recommended quotes that best fit the criteria below. Justify your choices in light of these criteria and any other criteria that seem appropriate:

- The quote advances the plot or is at a turning point.
- The quote reveals a main character.
- The quote contains strong imagery which adds to the atmosphere of the play.

	Justification for choice
First Choice Quote # _____	
Second Choice Quote # _____	

The nobler character:
Laertes or Hamlet?

Critical Challenge

Critical Question

Does Laertes or Hamlet show greater nobility of character?

Overview

Shakespeare frequently employed character foils in his plays. A foil can be defined as a character who, by contrast with the protagonist, underscores or enhances the distinctive characteristics of the protagonist. The focus in this critical challenge is on *Hamlet,* in particular Laertes (Ophelia's brother) and Hamlet. Students examine which of Laertes' circumstances are similar to those of Hamlet, and how the two characters react differently to similar circumstances. They consider the features of noble behaviour and then decide whether Hamlet or Laertes is portrayed as having the nobler character.

Requisite Tools

Background knowledge	• familiarity with selected scenes from *Hamlet*, in which Laertes and Hamlet appear
	• understand a character foil
Criteria for judgment	• features of a noble character (e.g. acts with honour, rises above petty matters
Critical thinking vocabulary	• inference
Thinking strategies	• data chart
Habits of mind	• open minded

Suggested Activities

◆ Introduce the concept of dramatic character construction using techniques such as character monologue, action and discussion by other characters. Explain how character traits are inferred from a character's words or actions. Offer as an example that an airplane crash survivor in the wilderness who complains about the difficulties of keeping his hair from looking windblown could be characterized as superficial, insecure or vain.

inference

◆ Introduce or review the concept of a character foil: a character whose circumstances are in some ways similar to those of the protagonist, but who reacts to them differently. A character foil is a way for the author to highlight, through contrast, certain character traits of the protagonist. Ask students to provide examples of character foils from other Shakespearean plays. Identify similarities between Laertes' and Hamlet's circumstances and the ways they react to these circumstances.

character foil

◆ In class discussion, identify and list traits they would expect to find in a noble character. This discussion should acknowledge and clarify the ambiguity inherent in the definition of the term "noble", which can mean either "of aristocratic birth" or "exalted in character." If time permits, ask students to generate plausible explanations of the genesis of such an ambiguity; during this discussion, it might be interesting to introduce the concept of *noblesse oblige*.

features of a noble character

◆ Assign students to work in groups of three or four to complete *Data Chart: Inferring Character Traits* (Blackline Master) recording significant words and actions of Hamlet or Laertes and listing character traits inferred from these words and actions.

data chart

Because *Hamlet* is a lengthy play, and Hamlet appears or is mentioned in almost every scene, it may be practical to have one group analyze Laertes' character (especially I, ii; I, iii; IV, vii; V, ii), and several groups analyze Hamlet's character as revealed at certain points in the play. (One group might be assigned Act I, another Act II and so forth.)

character of Hamlet and Laertes

Assign students to work in small groups to compare their data charts, noting differences in interpretation and discussing the reasoning that underlies their inferences about the characters' personalities.

◆ After small-group discussion, ask representatives from each group to present their findings and interpretations to the class and follow this activity with an open class discussion.

Summarize these findings using an the overhead projector and ask students to add information from other groups to their own data charts.

◆ Students are to use this accumulated information about the character traits of Laertes and Hamlet as the raw material for a two- or three-page essay that answers the following critical question:

> Does Laertes or Hamlet show greater nobility of character?

Explain that their essay should include the following:

- a clearly stated thesis which answers this question;

- consideration of the foil—character relationship between Laertes and Hamlet presented and an explanation of how this strengthens the conclusion;

- discussion of three or four traits that most strongly support the thesis;

- evidence that the opposing point of view has been considered (i.e., shows open mindedness).

Evaluation

◆ Use *Assessment Sheet: Hamlet/Laertes Character Essay* (Blackline Master) to evaluate student essays on the following criteria:

- degree to which the thesis is supported by the inferred character traits;

- degree to which inferences are supported by cited quotations;

- consideration of the concept of *character foil;*

- degree of consideration of multiple interpretations;

- strength of essay structure;

- quality of written expression.

Extension

◆ Invite students to write, in either blank verse or prose, "Laertes' soliloquy," to be inserted into the play at the end of IV, vii (when Laertes learns that his sister Ophelia's madness has led to her drowning). In this soliloquy, he ponders his present situation and his possible courses of action. Suggest that students use as a model Hamlet's "To be or not to be" soliloquy, (III, i, 56–88).

◆ Assign students to write a paragraph describing and explaining how Hamlet would have acted in the confrontation scene with Claudius (IV, v), if he were in Laertes' situation.

Inferring character traits

Character _____

EVIDENCE Act/scene/line(s)	EVIDENCE What the character says or does	CONCLUSION From this evidence, I infer that the character is . . .
I, ii, 50-56	Asks Claudius's permission to return to his studies in France; "Dread my lord . . ."	respectful (of the King's authority)

Data Chart

Hamlet/Laertes character essay

	weak		satisfactory		strong
Critical Analysis					
Character traits support thesis	1	2	3	4	5
Character traits supported by quotations	1	2	3	4	5
Inferred character traits from quotations are plausible	.5	1	1.5	2	2.5
Addresses foil character concept adequately	.5	1	1.5	2	2.5
Alternative interpretations of evidence have been considered	.5	1	1.5	2	2.5
Structure					
Clearly stated thesis	.5	1	1.5	2	2.5
Complete, well- structured introduction	.5	1	1.5	2	2.5
Individual paragraph structure	.5	1	1.5	2	2.5
Complete and well structured conclusion	.5	1	1.5	2	2.5
Balanced overall development	.5	1	1.5	2	2.5
Quality of Written Expression					
Mechanical correctness	1	2	3	4	5
Clear writing and forceful expression	1	2	3	4	5

Total   /40

Assessment Sheet

Honesty: Is it the best policy?

Critical Challenge

Critical Question

Is cheating always harmful to both the individual who cheats and the society to which he or she belongs?

Overview

Andrea Chisholm's essay "The 'High' of an Honest Win" examines the question of cheating, and more particularly, whether cheating is harmful to both the individual who cheats and the society to which he or she belongs. Students complete a pre-questionnaire on attitudes towards cheating, and then explore the meaning of the concept 'cheating.' They then read Chisholm's essay and explore the reasons for and against cheating.

Requisite Tools

Background knowledge	• understanding the concept 'cheating' • understanding the merits of not cheating
Criteria for judgment	
Critical thinking vocabulary	
Thinking strategies	• structuring a position paper
Habits of mind	• open-mindedness

Suggested Activities

◆ Inform students that the day's lesson focusses on an essay about cheating. Explain that, in order to gain insight into the general attitudes toward cheating, each student is asked to complete an anonymous questionnaire about cheating. Assure students that this questionnaire will be used only for general discussion purposes and not to judge anyone.

◆ Distribute a copy of *Student Activity #1: Questionnaire on Cheating* (Blackline Master) to each student. This fourteen-item questionnaire is designed to measure students' pre-lesson responses to assumptions and issues which Chisholm addresses in her essay on cheating. Ask students to write *on the back of the questionnaire* a secret number from 100 to 1000 which they must remember. The secret number allows students to get back their questionnaire without anyone else knowing which questionnaire belonged to which student.

◆ Collect the completed questionnaires and, to facilitate tabulation of data, redistribute them giving one completed questionnaire to each student. Proceed through each question having students indicate by raising their hand the response on the questionnaire before them. Count the hands raised for each option and record the tally for each question on an overheard prepared from *Transparency: Questionnaire Results* (Blackline Master). Confirm that students understand what the scores mean by asking students to interpret several of the results (e.g., if 19 of 27 responses to the comment "Everyone cheats sometimes" are "strongly agree," then what does this say about the prevalent attitude towards the frequency of cheating?). Invite students to share their reactions to the class results. Collect the questionnaires for later return to their authors.

◆ Organize students into groups of three or four, and invite them to complete *Student Activity #2: What Is Cheating?* (Blackline Master). Students are to discuss whether each of the ten actions listed is an example or a non-example of cheating. Each group, in effect, composes a definition of cheating by listing the key element of each action that caused them to classify it as either an example or non-example.

concept of cheating

◆ Invite each group to write their "definition"—i.e., their statements of the key elements—of cheating on the blackboard. As a class, discuss the differing statements and endeavour to reach consensus on a working definition of cheating for the purposes of this lesson.

◆ Ask students to read aloud Chisholm's essay, "The "High" of an Honest Win." Very briefly discuss the points raised in the essay.

◆ Working in their small groups, students are to consider the reasons for and against cheating by completing *Student Activity #3: Cheating—Why or Why Not?* (Blackline Master). Ask each group to attempt to reach consensus on which list of reasons is stronger and why. Invite groups to share their reasons and conclusions with the rest of the class.

merits of not cheating

◆ Using the secret numbers return the pre-lesson questionnaires to students. Invite them to re-examine their original responses to the questions in Part II (items 5 through 14). Discuss the notion of being open-minded—of not sticking to one's original position simply because that was what the person first thought, but of being willing to reconsider one's position in the face of new ideas. Encourage students who so desire to share any personal revelations.

open-mindedness

◆ Present the critical question:

> Is cheating always harmful to both the individual who cheats and the society to which he or she belongs?

Ask students to compose a response essay (position paper) that supports, modifies or refutes Chisholm's thesis. Suggest that students organize their brief essay according to the following structure:

structuring a position paper

Paragraph 1:   Briefly explain the issue, state their position on it, but do not present any reasons.

Paragraph 2:   Explain and support the reasons for their position.

Paragraph 3:   Identify reasons for a counter-position. Begin this paragraph with words like "On the other hand, some people believe." Offer any arguments that might be used to support their position against these counter-arguments.

Paragraph 4:   Compose a conclusion that refers back to the arguments and their position on the issue.

Evaluation

◆ Assess student essays on criteria such as the following:
- the essay considers opposing reasons;
- the essay offers a thoughtful justification for the conclusion reached;
- the essay correctly follows the required structure;
- correct spelling, punctuation and grammar.

Extension

◆ Using the same tabulation procedure with the post-lesson responses, compare any changes in group results between pre- and post-lesson responses. Discuss with the class the reasons for and significance of these changes, or lack of changes.

Reference

Chisholm, Andrea. (1992). "The 'High' of An Honest Win." In *Essays: Patterns and Perspectives*. Don Mills, ON: Oxford University Press.

Questionnaire on cheating

	strongly disagree	disagree	agree	strongly agree
Part I				
1. A study showed that 71 percent of students have copied homework to pass a homework check. Results would be about the same at my school.	1	2	3	4
2. The study showed that these same students had all attempted to find out test questions and answers from students who had previously written the test. Results would be about the same at my school.	1	2	3	4
3. The 71 percent of students who admitted to copying homework and attempting to find test questions and answers included many "A" students who had a reputation for being honest. Results would be about the same at my school.	1	2	3	4
4. These students justified their action with the reason, "It is just a survival tactic. Parents and teachers expect more from us than we can actually do." Comments would be about the same at my school.	1	2	3	4
Part II				
5. Everyone cheats sometimes.	1	2	3	4
6. When lots of people are cheating, I have to cheat too.	1	2	3	4
7. It is not a "big deal" to cheat on something small, such as a homework check, but it is wrong to cheat when money or awards are at stake.	1	2	3	4
8. Getting test questions or answers from someone else is not really cheating.	1	2	3	4
9. A little cheating in school is a necessary survival tool.	1	2	3	4
10. Nothing can be done about cheating.	1	2	3	4
11. All cheating is wrong.	1	2	3	4
12. All cheating results in negative consequences.	1	2	3	4
13. Cheating is harmful to the person who cheats.	1	2	3	4
14. Cheating is harmful to society.	1	2	3	4

Student Activity #1

Questionnaire results

	strongly disagree	disagree	agree	strongly agree
1. 71 percent of students have copied homework.				
2. Students had all attempted to find out test questions and answers.				
3. Students who copied/found test questions included many "A" students who had a reputation for being honest.				
4. Students justified their action with the reason, "It is just a survival tactic. . ."				
5. Everyone cheats sometimes.				
6. When lots of people are cheating, I have to cheat too.				
7. It is not a "big deal" to cheat on something small.				
8. Getting test questions or answers from someone else is not really cheating.				
9. A little cheating in school is a necessary survival tool.				
10. Nothing can be done about cheating.				
11. All cheating is wrong.				
12. All cheating results in negative consequences.				
13. Cheating is harmful to the person who cheats.				
14. Cheating is harmful to society.				

Transparency

What is cheating?

Indicate whether the following actions are an "example" or a "non-example" of cheating. Discuss the most important reason you used to classify each action. Use these reasons to help you come up with statements on the key elements of cheating. Record these elements in the space below the chart.

	Example of cheating	Non-example of cheating
1. committing a "good" foul in a basketball game		
2. asking someone who has already written a test for questions or answers		
3. copying some else's homework if it's not for marks		
4. "peeking" at a classmate's answers during a test		
5. getting some else to write a paper for you if you return the favour some time later		
6. being excused from taking a required course because you are a star college athlete		
7. telling a lie so that you won't get someone else in trouble		
8. watching someone cheat on a test and not reporting it		
9. copying a report out of a library book		
10. saying you need more time to complete an in-class essay so you can get help from someone else		

Key elements of cheating

Student Activity #2

Cheating—why and why not?

Reasons to cheat	Reasons not to cheat
1.	1.
2.	2.
3.	3.
4.	4.
5.	5.

Which set of reasons is stronger: to cheat or not to cheat? Why?

Student Activity #3

Punctuating "Galileo"?

Critical Challenge

Critical Tasks

Punctuate five sections of the song "Galileo" (performed by the Indigo Girls) and explain the punctuation.

Overview

The song "Galileo," performed by the Indigo Girls and written entirely in lower case letters without punctuation, presents students with a unique punctuation task. These factors make the song difficult to follow on paper; therefore, it is a wonderful example of the importance of punctuation. Students listen to the song to hear punctuation clues, add the necessary punctuation marks to the text of the song lyrics and then rewrite the lyrics with punctuation corrections.

Requisite Tools

Background knowledge	• knowledge of rules of capitalization, end punctuation, internal punctuation (i.e., commas, semi-colon, dash)
	• thought divisions (i.e., stanza breaks, paragraphs)
Criteria for judgment	• criteria for effective punctuation (e.g., clarity of meaning, integrity of ideas, highlighting independent ideas)
Critical thinking vocabulary	
Thinking strategies	
Habits of mind	• attention to detail

Suggested Activities

◆ Prior to starting, it may be useful to quickly review the basic rules of the punctuation to be used in this lesson. Establish a class set of criteria for judging when and why punctuation is needed (e.g., to clarify meaning, to recognize independent ideas).

punctuation, thought divisions capitalization

◆ Present the first part of the critical task:

> Punctuate the song "Galileo" performed by the Indigo Girls.

◆ Play the song for the class. Advise students to listen to the natural pauses in the song's phrasing for punctuation clues. Direct students to add punctuation as they read along while listening to the song. It will likely be necessary to play the song at least twice.

◆ Distribute *Student Activity: Punctuating "Galileo"* (Blackline Master) containing the unpunctuated lyrics to "Galileo" by the Indigo Girls.

◆ Ask students to review the lyrics without listening to them and consider their editing of the lyrics for punctuation.

attention to detail

◆ Organize students into pairs or small groups to discuss decisions about punctuation. Assign groups a portion of the song to present to the class in punctuated form. Distribute acetate sheets and using an overhead projector is an effective way to make this presentation.

criteria for effective punctuation

◆ During the presentation, ask other groups to debate editorial decisions made by each group. Discuss the subtleties of punctuation and variations. Review criteria which can be used to decide about the use of punctuation.

◆ Listen to the song one final time and ask students to discuss how different punctuations of the song produces different meanings. Conclude the lesson with a discussion about the importance of punctuation.

◆ Present the second half of the critical task:

> As individuals, students select five portions of the text of the song into which they introduce punctuation, enter these and the punctuation on the ?

> Encourage students to illustrate their answers with examples from the song.

Evaluation

◆ Write an essay about the importance that punctuation has on meaning. Use examples.

◆ Evaluate the chart using the following criteria (and/or others decided on in class)

- embodies principles of punctuation;
- embodies a plausible interpretation of the song;
- offers plausible reason for the punctuation;
- offers plausible explanation of the way (or ways) in which lack of punctuation could be misleading or confusing;
- offers examples from the song which illustrate the criteria listed above.

◆ Evaluate students' essays on the following criteria:
- understanding of rules for use of punctuation;
- the ways punctuation can affect meaning;
- clarity of ideas;
- number and richness of examples to support/illustrate content of the essay;
- effective punctuation.

Extension

◆ Discuss the message of the song — the desire to seek the deep truths of our lives — alluding to the references to the astronomer Gallileo's ability to uncover the workings of the universe.

Punctuating "Galileo"

Just before going to press we learned that we could not acquire the rights to duplicate the lyrics for Galileo.

A punctuated version of the lyrics for this song is on the Web at:

http://www.lifeblood.net/lyrics/athruz/galileo.html

Other popular songs could be substituted by preparing an unpunctuated draft for students to punctuate.

Student Activity #1

Punctuating "Galileo"

SECTION 1 (text from song, punctuated):

Explain how your punctuation affects interpretation:

Explain how your punctuation clarifies the text:

SECTION 2 (text from song, punctuated):

Explain how your punctuation affects interpretation:

Explain how your punctuation clarifies the text:

SECTION 3 (text from song, punctuated):

Explain how your punctuation affects interpretation:

Explain how your punctuation clarifies the text:

Student Activity #2

page 1 of 2

SECTION 4 (text from song, punctuated):

Explain how your punctuation affects interpretation:

Explain how your punctuation clarifies the text:

SECTION 5 (text from song, punctuated):

Explain how your punctuation affects interpretation:

Explain how your punctuation clarifies the text:

On the other hand

Critical Challenge

Critical Task

Rewrite a classic fairy tale from the point of view of someone other than that found in the traditional version.

Overview

Students are read a revised version of a classic fairy tale—possibly *The Frog Prince - Continued* (Jon Scieszka's remake of "The Frog Prince") or *The True Story of the Three Little Pigs by A. Wolf* (Jon Scieszka's remake of "The Three Little Pigs"). After discussing the notion of point of view and the techniques used to alter point of view, students identify criteria of an effective "rewrite" of a fairy tale. Each student then selects a classic fairy tale and rewrites the story from a secondary character's point of view.

Requisite Tools

Background knowledge	• familiarity with the traditional and revised versions of a classic fairy tale	
Criteria for judgment	• features of a successful "re-write" (e.g., believable, empathic, inclusive, imaginative, authentic, etc.)	
Critical thinking vocabulary	• point of view	
Thinking strategies	• data chart	
Habits of mind	• role empathy	

Suggested Activities

◆ Announce that you are about to read to the class a revised version of a classic fairy tale. Begin reading either *The Frog Prince - Continued* by Jon Scieszka (a remake of "The Frog Prince") or *The True Story of the Three Little Pigs by A. Wolf* also by Jon Scieszka (a remake of "The Three Little Pigs").

familiarity with fairy tales

◆ After reading the revised fairy tale, arrange students in groups of four or five to discuss the differences between the original and the revised versions. Encourage students to explore the ranges of differences—in interpretations of motive, character identification, description of events, outcome, etc.—arising from the telling of the story from a secondary character's point of view. Invite students to share the results of their group discussions with the rest of class. Ensure that all students understand that the revised version has shifted the point of view from which the tale is normally told.

point of view

◆ In a class discussion using the chalkboard or in small groups, ask students to brainstorm key features of a successful "point of view" rewrite of a fairy tale. The following criteria seem especially relevant for consideration:

features of a successful re-write

- *believable*: the reinterpretation is credible/plausible;

- *empathic*: sensitively captures other character's perspective/feelings/outlook;

- *inclusive*: accounts for all of the events in the original tale;

- *imaginative*: offers a fresh/novel re-interpretation of the characters' motives and thinking;

- *authentic*: is written in the language, tone and style of the original fairy tale.

◆ After the class has discussed and agreed upon a common list of criteria for a successful rewrite, ask them to discuss within their groups how successfully the revised fairy tale they have just heard meets these criteria. It may be helpful to have a traditional version of the fairy tale available for students to consult. You may wish to make this a more formal assignment. If so, distribute *Student Activity: A Successful Rewrite* (Blackline Master), or a similar activity sheet listing the criteria that the class generated for students to use in assessing the success of the revised version of the fairy tale.

◆ Ask students to share their assessments with the rest of the class, encouraging them to support their conclusions with references from the text.

◆ After a brief class discussion on the degree of success of the re-write of the fairy tale, present the critical task:

Rewrite a classic fairy tale from the point of view of someone other than the traditional perspective.

Begin by brainstorming the titles of other fairy tales that might lend themselves to adaptation or continuation from the perspective of another character in the story. Decide whether all students will rewrite the same fairy tale, or whether students will make their own selection. Encourage students to study the classic version before beginning the task. Remind students to consider the criteria for an effective rewrite as they complete the assignment.

Evaluation

◆ If used, assess the *Student Activity* sheet on the following criteria:

- amount of explanation offered for each assessment;
- relevance of the explanation to the criteria being assessed;
- adequacy of the explanation in supporting the assessment rendered.

◆ Assess the students' revised fairy tale on the basis of how well the agreed-upon criteria have been met. If desired, add additional literary criteria (e.g., clarity of prose, use of imagery, rich descriptive language) and technical criteria (e.g., correct spelling, punctuation and grammar).

◆ The *Student Activity* sheet may be used if the assignment is to be peer- or self-assessed.

Extension

◆ If students are familiar with the "writing process"—prewriting, drafting, editing, revising, publishing and presenting—suggest that, working in small groups, they proceed through each of the steps, beginning with a prewriting exercise where they share ideas with one another prior to settling down to write a rough draft.

◆ In groups of four or five, arrange for students to read each other's revised fairy tales and to nominate which one of them is the most effective given the agreed-upon criteria. You may wish to use *Student Activity: A Successful Rewrite* (Blackline Master), or a similar activity sheet, listing the criteria that the class generated for students to use in assessing the most successfully re-written fairy tale. Present each group's nomination to the entire class who then will judge the three best re-written classics.

◆ Invite students to prepare an illustrated version of their fairy tale to share with their fellow students or with an elementary class.

◆ Drawing from an anthology of short stories, select and read a story which lends itself to further discussion of point of view. It may be useful to further refine students' notion of point of view to include first-person narrative, second-person narrative and omniscient narrator. Students might select a passage from the story and rewrite it from two other narrative perspectives.

References

Scieszka, Jon. (1991). *The Frog Prince - Continued.* New York: Viking.

A successful rewrite

On a scale of 1 to 4, indicate how successfully each criterion has been met.
Explain your assessment, including references to the text.

4 = Outstanding   3 = Good   2 = Satisfactory   1 = Weak

Criteria for a successful re-write		Explanation for assessment
believable: the re-interpretation is credible/plausible	4 3 2 1	
empathic: sensitively captures secondary character's perspective/feelings/outlook	4 3 2 1	
inclusive: accounts for all of the events in the original tale	4 3 2 1	
imaginative: offers a fresh re-interpretation of the secondary character's motives and thinking	4 3 2 1	
authentic: is written in the language, tone and style of the original fairy tale	4 3 2 1	
	4 3 2 1	
	4 3 2 1	

Overall assessment: 4 = Outstanding   3 = Good   2 = Satisfactory   1 = Weak